IMPORTANT NOTE:

VISIT WWW.EMMAUS-WAY.COM/FMTJ-NEWS

FOR ADDITIONAL INFORMATION AND

UPDATES TO THIS BOOK

Related books from Emmaus Way LLC

The Pivotal Pastor

A richly detailed story about how a small country parish (St. Mary at Fremont Center) expanded their campus and faith community at the turn of the century. Fr. Ron Lewinski arrived in 1996 as the new pastor. Through his vision and leadership, a new church was built and the number of ministries expanded from a handful to over three dozen when the new church was dedicated six years later. The architect was world-renowned Dirk Lohan, whose work includes expansions to Adler Planetarium and the Shedd Acquarium in Chicago. The book includes dozens of photographs from the project, which engaged descendants of families identified in "From Münk to Johnsburg."

Remembering Ron Lewinski

Rembrances of Fr. Lewinski, former pastor of St. Mary at Fremont Center, by clergy and laity who knew him. Indluded are Cardinal Blase Cupich (Archbishop of Chicago), Cardinal Wilton Gregory (Archbishop of Washington D.C.) and Bishop Franz-Peter Tebartz-van Elst of Germany (Curia-Bishop in the Vatican).

Rosa's Little Book of Recipes

This book was inspired by the hand-written recipes of Rosa C. Kennebeck, wife of Henry Kennebeck. It is a tribute by her son David Kennebeck, publisher of "From Münk to Johnsburg." Each recipe is accompanied by a photograph of a family memory, spanning the years from 1902 through 2010. Several photos are of people named in "From Münk to Johnsburg."

Visit www.emmaus-way.com/shop

From Münk to Johnsburg

The Jacob Schmitt & Anna Goedert Family

A Founding Family of St. John the Baptist Church and Johnsburg, Illinois

Compiled by Sandie L. Schwarz

Maternal 3x great-granddaughter of Jacob & Anna Schmitt

Emmaus Way LLC

First Edition

Copyright 2024 Sandie L. Schwarz. The compiler claims copyright only for those portions of this work that are original content. The compiler recognizes this work is assembled from content created by others and makes no claims to those rights, and intends no infringement. Wherever possible, credit has been given to the originator.

ISBN: 979-8-9866668-3-9 (print)

If this is an electronic version (PDF) of the book, the compiler and publisher have provided it to you without Digital Rights Management software (DRM) applied so that you can enjoy reading it on your personal devices. This PDF is for your personal use only. You may not print or post this PDF or make this e-book publicly available in any way.

CIP DATA
Names: Schwarz, Sandie L., compiler.
Title: From Münk to Johnsburg : the Jacob Schmitt & Anna Goedert family , a founding family of Johnsburg Illinois / compiled by Sandie L. Schwarz.
Description: Includes bibliographical references and index. | Brooksville, FL: Emmaus Way LLC, 2024.
Identifiers: ISBN: 979-8-9866668-3-9
Subjects: LCSH Schmitt family. | Goedert family. | German Americans—Illinois--History. | German Americans--Johnsburg--Illinois. | Johnsburg (Ill.)--History. | Johnsburg (Ill.)--Genealogy. | St. John the Baptist Catholic Church (Johnsburg, Ill.) | BISAC HISTORY / United States / 19th Century | HISTORY / United States / 20th Century | HISTORY / United States / 21st Century | HISTORY / United States / State & Local / Midwest (IA, IL, IN, KS, MI, MN, MO, ND, NE, OH, SD, WI) | HISTORY / Europe / Germany
Classification: LCC BX4603.J587 F76 2024 | DDC 929/.377322--dc23

Cover and book design by David J. Kennebeck
Photographs are from family and public archives. Professional photographers took some photos. Photo of St. John the Baptist Church on the title page is from 1940.

Several photographs have been restored using Artificial Intelligence (www.fotor.com) and/or edited using GIMP (and the editor's personal artificial intelligence). The manuscript was prepared using Scrivener on Mac.

Neither the publisher nor the compiler is responsible for content that may change at the locations of the web pages referenced in this book that are the responsibility of other entities.

We realize that "gremlins" have clever ways of hiding within a book. We've tried to root them out; but should you find any factual, grammatical, spelling, or punctuation errors we would very much like you to bring it to our attention. Just send an email with the details to "info@emmaus-way" with a subject line of GREMLIN JACOB SCHMITT. Our sincere thanks!

Published by Emmaus Way LLC.
Printed in the U.S.A. 241206

First Print Edition 2024
1 2 3 4 5 6 7 8 9 10 11 12

Contents

Preface	1
Acknowledgements	3
Introduction	6
I Jacob Schmitt (1808-1892)	11
II Susanna Goedert-Schmitt (1832-1910)	15
III Anna Maria Schmitt (1834-1854)	73
IV Gertrud Schmitt (1839-1902)	77
V Nicholas Schmitt (1841-1929)	119
VI Peter Schmitt (1848-1883)	153
Index	163
Reader's Notes	

This book is dedicated to those members of the Jacob Schmitt family who have gone before us leaving a heritage of fortitude, faith and families.

Preface

I started to research my family ancestry, beginning with my maternal ancestry, in 2002. At that time, I only had knowledge of who my grandparents were, and who one of my great-grandparents was, being Elizabeth SCHAEFER KENNEBECK.

It was only a matter of time before I discovered that Jacob SCHMITT, a founder of Johnsburg, was my 3x great-grandfather. This occurred when I was on a mission to identify the parents of my great-grandmother Elizabeth. They being, Nicholas SCHAEFER and Gertrude SCHMITT, a daughter of Jacob SCHMITT and Anna GOEDERT.

Further research led to discovering — to my surprise — that Jacob SCHMITT (1808-1892) was one of three founders of what became known as Johnsburg in McHenry County, Illinois. Jacob, along with Nicolaus ADAMS (1799-1879) and Nicolaus FRETT (1795-1844), were the first families who founded the town of Johnsburg and were founders of St. John the Baptist Catholic Church in Johnsburg.

Local church records are the main source I used for the Jacob SCHMITT family and their descendants. Also, county courthouse records and The McHenry Plaindealer newspaper.

— Sandie L. Schwarz
September, 2024

Acknowledgements

Special thanks to family researchers Teryl "Terry" MILLER (1939-2020) and Gary ANDERSON for providing data from the church records in Germany. Terry, a paternal descendent of the Nikolaus Muller (1780-1859) family (surname was Americanized to Mueller and Miller by descendants) family from Langenfeld, who were early settlers of Johnsburg in 1846, often traveled to Germany visiting the villages and churches. He was able to access the church books that recorded the marriages, births and deaths of family members. He also spent many years viewing the LDS microfilm of the church records, transcribing and publishing several books. He compiled, then had published, the book *From Langenfeld to Johnsburg* in 2008, recording his Mueller/Miller ancestry. The Miller family continues to hold a Miller reunion annually in October at the Miller Chapel in Johnsburg. Terry would also visit the Newberry Library in Chicago. During one visit he discovered the photo of Jacob and Anna, in a German newspaper (see Chapter I). At the time of his death, Terry was working on completing books for his FREUND family research, a church record book for St. Quirinus Catholic Church in Langenfeld, and a book that was to contain the families and their descendants, of the Early Settlers of Johnsburg.

Gary ANDERSON, while living and working in Germany before retiring and returning to the United States in 2014, traveled to many of the same villages and churches. He recorded from their archives the marriages, births and deaths of family members. Gary is a maternal descendent of the NIKOLAUS JUSTEN (1813-1902) family, early settlers of Johnsburg in 1854. Gary has compiled a

ACKNOWLEDGEMENTS

booklet titled "THE IMMIGRANT FOUNDERS, MEMBERS and ASSOCIATES OF SAINT JOHN THE BAPTIST CATHOLIC CHURCH, JOHNSBURG, ILLINOIS."

Special thanks to family researcher Vern PADDOCK, a 3x great-grandson of Jacob SCHMITT, through daughter Susanna SCHMITT (Johann MUELLER), for many of the photos of his ancestors, descendants of his 2x great-grandmother Susanna SCHMITT MUELLER. I first learned of my connection to Vern, when I was on the Find A Grave website (www.findagrave.com). I saw his name as being the manager of the Jacob SCHMITT memorial. Having no idea at the time that Vern was related to Jacob Schmitt, I emailed him asking to please transfer the memorial to me, as Jacob Schmitt is my 3x great-grandfather. Vern kindly replied that no, he would not transfer because Jacob Schmitt was also his 3x great-grandfather. I was pleasantly surprised to discover our connection and I settled for sponsoring Jacob SCHMITT'S memorial, thereby removing the ads from the memorial page that Ancestry.com normally presents.

Thank You to Marjorie Beiser (Fred) nee Budach, a granddaughter of Mary SCHMITT (Peter ARNOLDI). Some of the many Nicholas Schmitt family photos she sent me appear in this book.

Thank you to Susanne Nestor Heron, for the wedding photo of her grandparents, Nicholas Kennebeck & Laura Scheid.

A Very Special Thank You to my uncle, Dave Kennebeck, for his support while editing and publishing this book. He has taken my years of our Jacob Schmitt family research and invested a good share of his own time to make this family book possible.

Additional sources include:

- Important resources from the local libraries including the Johnsburg Library; McHenry Library Genealogy Room

ACKNOWLEDGEMENTS

reference materials, including micro film of census records and the McHenry Plaindealer, now also digitized; McHenry County Genealogical Society resources; McHenry County, Historical Society Research Library in Union, Illinois; McHenry County Courthouse records, Woodstock, Illinois.

- Ship Passenger List, microfilm accessed through The Genealogy Center at Allen County Public Library, Ft. Wayne, Indiana.
- St. Stephan Catholic Church records, in Nachtsheim, Mayen, Rhineland, Germany.
- St. Kastor Catholic Church records in Münk, Mayen, Rhineland, Germany.
- St. Kastor Parish, Weiler, Kreis Mayen, Germany; Author: Teryl Miller (Compiler) Summary: Catholic Church records from Latter Day Saints microfilms of the original records of the St. Kastor Catholic Church, Weiler, Kreis Mayen, Germany. It includes brief history of church, baptism, marriage, confirmation, death and immigration records from 1682-1870. https://www.worldcat.org/title/St.-Kastor- parish-Weiler-Kreis-Mayen-Germany/oclc/1041112457.
- St. John the Baptist Catholic Church records, Johnsburg, McHenry County, Illinois.
- Transcribed church records by the McHenry County Illinois Genealogical Society (MCIGS). Volumes I 1852-1868, II 1869-1882 and III 1883-1909 of Early Records of St. John the Baptist Catholic Church are available at local libraries including Johnsburg Public Library, McHenry Public Library, Crystal Lake Public Library, Richmond Public Library and Woodstock Public Library.

Lastly, the reader can expect to see various spellings for a surname — and also a given name — throughout the book. These names have been found recorded with variations in their spellings.

INTRODUCTION

The Jacob SCHMITT family records going back to 1705 (when today's Germany was a part of the Holy Roman Empire) are recorded at St. Stephan Catholic Church in Parish of Nachtsheim in Nachtsheim, Mayen, Rhineland, Germany. Jacob and Anna nee GOEDERT were married on 12 February 1833 at St. Alban Catholic Church in Naunheim, Mayen, Rhineland, Prussia (today Germany).

Jacob SCHMITT was born in Münk, Mayen, Rhineland, Prussia (today Germany) in what is known as the Eifel Region, on 30 March 1808, the 6th of 10 known children born to Michael SCHMITT (1769-1817) and Catharina BELL (1777-bet 1844 and 1850). Today Münk is a municipality in the District of Mayen-Koblenz in the northwestern section of the state of Rhineland-Palatinate, Western Germany, the Eifel region. It is a mountainous region with volcanic lakes, forests and vineyards. Population: (December 2022) Total 262. Collective municipality is Vordereifel.

THE MÜNK COAT OF ARMS

INTRODUCTION

When Jacob SCHMITT and his family immigrated to America, the Rhineland area was poor, having suffered from famine and crop failures. Jacob SCHMITT was the first member of his family to come to America, arriving at Port of New York on 2 August 1841. Jacob SCHMITT, one of three founders of Johnsburg, and his family, were accompanied by the Nicolaus ADAMS (1799-1879) and Nicolaus FRETT (1785-1844) families. These three families were the first to settle in what became Johnsburg in McHenry County, Illinois. They founded St. John the Baptist Catholic Church.

"The first log cabin church built in 1842 served also as a school and meeting hall until 1850 when a larger frame church was built. Over the next eighteen years the parish grew both in numbers and in its commitment to God, and in 1867 a third church was begun. Built in the Gothic style so popular in Germany, this beautiful church took thirteen years to complete and was the pride of the Johnsburg community until it was tragically destroyed by fire on February 19, 1900. The church was rebuilt on the original site in its original gothic style with the traditional interior. This beautiful church has continued to serve since those early days."

ST. JOHN THE BAPTIST CHURCH, EXTERIOR

INTRODUCTION

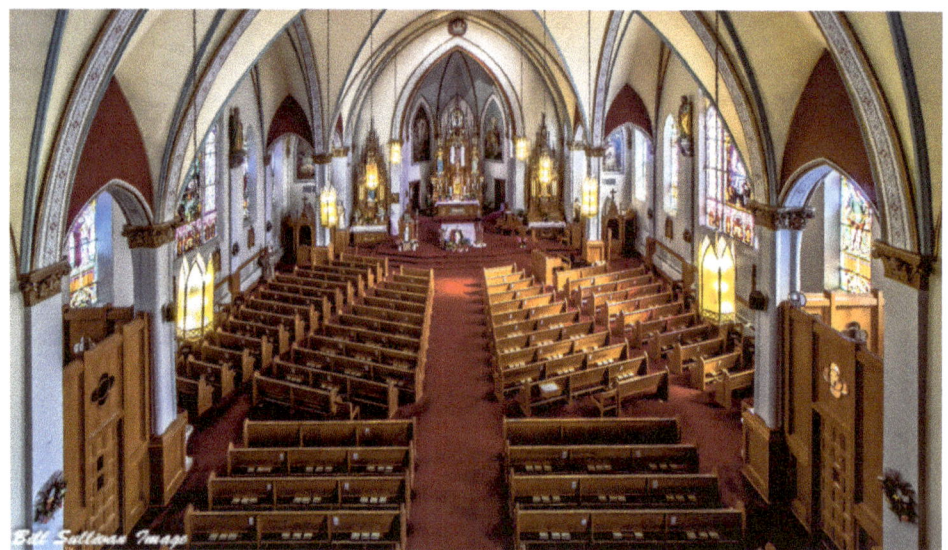

ST. JOHN THE BAPTIST CHURCH, INTERIOR

FOUNDER'S PLAQUES HONORING FOUNDING FAMILIES OF ADAMS, FRETT & SCHMITT:

INTRODUCTION

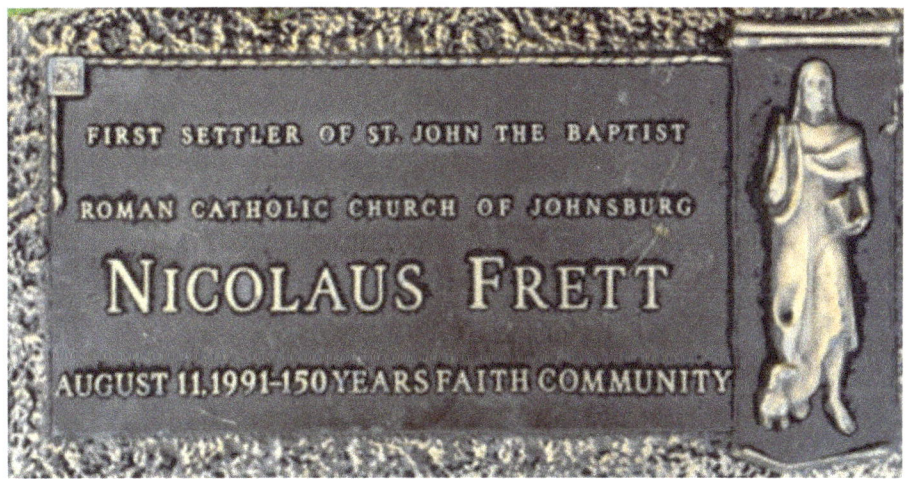

CHRONOLOGY OF IMMIGRATION

Port of New York Arrivals with Passenger List, found to date, for the five surviving children (and their families) of Catharina nee Bell and Michael Schmitt, and also a brother of Catharina, Johann Peter Bell, all of whom immigrated to America and came to

INTRODUCTION

Johnsburg, including Catharina who we think arrived with her son Friedrich:

1) Jacob Schmitt (Anna Goedert) arrived 2 August 1841, aboard the ship *Albany*.

2) Friedrich Schmitt (Anna Schaefer) arrived about June 1842 per his Declaration of Intent, filed at Woodstock Circuit Court, Woodstock, McHenry County, Illinois.

3) Johann Peter Bell, brother of Catharina Schmitt nee Bell, (3. Maria Halfmann) arrived 20 August 1842, aboard the ship *Navigator*.

4) Johann Peter Schmitt (Gertrud Schaefer) arrived 11 July 1843, aboard the ship *Infatigable*.

5) Susanna Schmitt (1. Nicolas Meurer) arrived 11 July 1843 aboard the ship *Infatigable*.

6) Maria C. Schmitt (2. Michael Pulvermacher) arrived 24 July 1854, aboard the ship *Phantom*.

It has been my privilege to compile this ancestral collection. I invite you to advise me of any corrections or additions via an email to info@emmaus-way.com with a subject line of ATTN: SANDIE SCHWARZ.

Chapter I

THE DESCENDANTS OF
JACOB SCHMITT AND ANNA GOEDERT

*(Children, Grandchildren, Great-Grandchildren
& Great-Great Grandchildren)*

Jacob Schmitt along with his wife Anna (nee Goedert) and their children, Susanna age 9, Anna Maria age 7, Michael age 5 and Gertrud age 2, emigrated from Münk and departed from Port of Le Havre, France. Jacob Schmitt, along with Nicolaus Adams (1799-1879) and Nicolaus Frett (1795-1844) were the first three families who founded the town of Johnsburg in McHenry County, Illinois.

The three families began their journey from Port of Le Havre, France. They sailed for 38 days to reach New York, arriving at Port of New York on 2 August 1841 aboard the ship *Albany*. They traveled from New York to Chicago by train. From Chicago they journeyed by oxen-drawn wagon to what became the Village of Johnsburg. Jacob's wife Anna was with child on their journey across the Atlantic Ocean to America. Their son Nicholas Schmitt was born 2 months after their arrival, on 7 October 1841. Nicholas was the first child to be born in what became Johnsburg.

The following Chapters record each of the children of Jacob & Anna who lived to adulthood and their descendants, up to and including, Jacob & Anna's great and great-great grandchildren. (There is no chapter for Michael. He was five years old when he immigrated with his parents. We do not know where or when he died, only that he was not recorded with his family in the 1850 Census.)

Between their five surviving children, Jacob & Anna had 47 grandchildren, 126 great-grandchildren and 303 great-great grandchildren Their great-great granddaughter MARGARET MARY TEKAMPE PADDOCK, passed on 19 November 2017 at the age of 101 years, a Centenarian. Margaret was the great-granddaughter of Jacob & Anna's daughter Susanna Goedert-Schmitt Müller (Mueller). An ancestry of the Jacob Schmitt family, and descendants — created by the Compiler of this volume — can be viewed online at WikiTree:
https://www.wikitree.com/wiki/Schmitt-2383

JACOB SCHMITT AND ANNA GOEDERT
(NEWSPRINT PHOTO CIRCA MID-1800S)

1. JACOB SCHMITT Born on 30 March 1808 in Münk, Dist. Mayen, Rhineland, Prussia (Germany), the son of MICHAEL

SCHMITT (1769-1817) & CATHARINA BELL (1777-bet 1844 and 1850). Catharina also came to America. She died in Johnsburg between 1844 and 1850. JACOB SCHMITT died in Johnsburg, McHenry County, Illinois on 7 September 1892. Burial at St. John the Baptist Cemetery in Johnsburg. Jacob Schmitt's year of death is recorded in a Jacob Schmitt family list created between 1904 and 1910, by the granddaughter of Jacob Schmitt, (daughter of Jacob's son Nicholas Schmitt), Katherine Schmitt, and her mother Maria Meiler Schmitt. This list can be viewed upon request at the Brown County Historical Society in Minnesota. A Founder's Plaque was placed at the gravesite of Jacob Schmitt by the McHenry County Historical Society in 1991.
https://www.findagrave.com/memorial/75470838/jacob-schmitt

FOUNDER'S PLAQUE AT JACOB SCHMITT'S GRAVESITE

On 12 February 1833, JACOB SCHMITT married ANNA GERTRUD GOEDERT, daughter of WILHELM GOEDERT (1771-1835) & MARIA GERTRUD MOHR (1775-1851), at St. Alban Catholic Church in Naunheim, Dist. Mayen, Rhineland, Prussia. ANNA GERTRUD GOEDERT was born on 2 August 1806 in Naunheim, Dist. Mayen, Rhineland, Prussia. Anna died in Johnsburg, McHenry County, Illinois on 16 May 1882. Burial at St.

John the Baptist Cemetery in Johnsburg.
https://www.findagrave.com/memorial/75470945/anna_gertrude_schmitt

ANNA GOEDERT obit in the **McHenry Plaindealer, 24 May 1882, page 5**:

> *"The mother of Peter Smith, who keeps the McHenry House, died at her residence near Johnsburgh, one day last week. She was seventy-eight years of age and one of the oldest settlers in this section."*

JACOB & ANNA were the parents of:

2. i. SUSANNA GOEDERT-SCHMITT MUELLER (1832-1910)
3. ii. ANNA MARIA SCHMITT FREUND (1834-1854)
4. iii. MICHAEL SCHMITT (1836-aft August 1841, bef 1850)
5. iv. GERTRUD SCHMITT SCHAEFER (1839-1902)
6. v. NICHOLAS SCHMITT (1841-1929)
7. vi. PETER SCHMITT (SMITH) (1848-1883)

Note: In the original birth record for daughter SUSANNA, it appears that she may not be a biological daughter of JACOB SCHMITT. Susanna was born five months before Jacob & Anna married and she was baptized 'SUSANNA GOEDERT.'

Descendants of JACOB SCHMITT & ANNA GOEDERT
Chapters II-VI:
48 Grandchildren (Bold Black)
126 Great-grandchildren (Fuchsia)
303 2x Great-grandchildren (Teal)

Chapter II

SUSANNA GOEDERT-SCHMITT

2. SUSANNA GOEDERT Born on 27 September 1832 in Naunheim, Dist. Mayen, Rhineland, Prussia (today Germany). Susanna was 9 years of age at the time she and her parents Jacob and Anna, and her siblings, Anna Maria age 7, Michael age 5 and Gertrud age 2, immigrated to America. Her mother Anna was with child on the ocean crossing to America, and she gave birth to a son Nicholas on 7 October 1841, the first child to be born in Johnsburg. The family departed from Port of Le Havre, France. They sailed for 38 days to reach New York, arriving at Port of New York on 2 August 1841 aboard the ship *Albany*. They traveled from New York to Chicago by train. From Chicago they journeyed by oxen-drawn wagon to what became the Village of Johnsburg. The Jacob Schmitt family traveled with the families of Nicolaus Adams (1799-1879) and Nicolaus Frett (1795-1844). They were the first three families, all from Dist. Mayen, Rhineland, Prussia who founded the town of Johnsburg in McHenry County, Illinois.

Susanna died at the home of her daughter Emma Kennebeck (2nd wife of John Henry) in McHenry, McHenry County, Illinois on 19 October 1910. Burial 22 October 1910 at St. Mary's Catholic Cemetery in McHenry:
https://www.findagrave.com/memorial/71757631/susanna-mueller

Obituary in McHenry Plaindealer, 27 October 1910, Front page.

AN EARLY SETTLER DEAD

MRS. SUSANNA MUELLER IS DEAD AT RIPE OLD AGE.

Came Here From Germany In the Early Forties and Was Among the First Three Families to Settle at Johnsburgh.

Just about an hour before the golden sunbeams were kissing the tree tops, bidding the sleepy world to awake and gird itself for a new and glorious day, the soul of one of McHenry's oldest as well as earliest settlers passed thru the golden gates to her heavenly reward, on Wednesday morning, Oct. 19, 1910,—the soul of Mrs. John Mueller.

The end came at the home of her daughter, Mrs. John H. Kennebeck, where she had been making her home for some time, death coming thru a general breakdown, which, on account of her advanced age, she was unable to withstand.

The subject of this sketch was born at Munk, Grais Maizen, R. G. Koblenz, Germany, Sept. 27, 1822. She obtained but very little schooling, as she was but nine years of age when her parents and the balance of the family sailed the ocean of waters to the new world, America. Her parents were Mr. and Mrs. Jacob Schmitt. On the family's arrival in America they came direct to a point where Johnsburgh now stands, the Schmitt family being one of three then residing at that point, the other two families being those of Nicklous Adams and Nicklous Frett. With but three white families in that section of the country one can easily imagine existing conditions at that time. However, being of that sturdy, courageous stock, she, with the balance of the white settlers, set out to assist in making a livelihood.

The Schmitt homestead, a log cabin, stood on the site, or near to it, now occupied by the handsome Catholic church at Johnsburgh.

Miss Susanna Schmitt was united in marriage to Mr. John Mueller (deceased) in the year of 1849. A few years after her marriage her husband purchased the farm now owned by Nick F. Freund, near Johnsburgh, on which she continued to reside until about twelve years ago, when, with her husband and the children that were at home at the time, she moved to McHenry, which place was her place of abode up to the time of her death. The union was blessed with sixteen children, nine of whom with the husband preceded the deceased to the great beyond, while seven are living to share the sorrow her demise has brought them. The living children are as follows: William, Peter H. and Mrs. Josephine Mayer of Stacyville, Ia.; Mrs. Mary K. Lensen of Fremont, Ill.; John W. Mueller of Spring Grove, Ill.;

Mrs. John H. Kennebeck and Miss Elizabeth Mueller of this place. Besides the children she leaves forty-two grandchildren and twenty-three great-grandchildren.

Mrs. Mueller was a woman of a sweet and sympathetic nature and at all times was greatly devoted to her family. Her excellencies were beyond count, while her generous heart prompted her to fulfill more than a few acts of charity towards those in need. She led a life in strict adherence with the Roman Catholic faith, of which she was a faithful believer. No woman could set a better example for her children and the world than did she and her place can never again be filled in this world, where women of her calibre are so sadly needed. The deceased will be greatly missed by a circle of admiring friends, but her kind deeds while among us will never be forgotten.

The funeral took place from St. Mary's Catholic church here on Friday morning of last week and was largely attended. Rev. A. Royer, pastor of the church, officiated. The remains were laid to rest beside those of her husband in St. Mary's cemetery.

CARD OF THANKS.

The children of the late Mrs. Susanna Mueller wish in this manner to thank the many kind friends who extended helping and sympathetic hands during their recent sad bereavement.

NOTE: In the original St. Alban Catholic Church birth/ baptismal record for SUSANNA, it appears that she may not be a biological daughter of JACOB SCHMITT. SUSANNA was born before JACOB SCHMITT & ANNA GOEDERT married (Jacob & Anna married 5 months after the birth of Susanna) and SUSANNA was baptized 'SUSANNA GOEDERT'. Today, DNA testing of descendants may help to determine if JACOB SCHMITT was or was not SUSANNA GOEDERT'S biological father.

On 5 May 1849, SUSANNA GOEDERT-SCHMITT married JOHANN MÜLLER (MUELLER), son of NIKOLAUS MÜLLER (1780-1859) & ANNA KLEIN (1799-1860). Their marriage was recorded at St. Joseph Catholic Church in Wilmette, Cook County, Illinois. JOHANN MÜLLER was born on 18 June 1821 in Langenfeld, Dist. Mayen, Rhineland, Prussia and baptized on 21 June 1821 at St. Quirinus Catholic Church in Langenfeld, Mayen, Rhineland, Prussia. He emigrated with his parents Nikolaus (1780-1859) and Anna Catharina (nee Klein) (1799-1860) MÜLLER (MUELLER) and siblings, Peter (1824-1863) and Maria Catharina (1821-1911), emigrated from Prussia (today Germany) in April-May of 1847. They settled first in Westphalia, Michigan, May of 1847, before coming to Johnsburg, McHenry County, Illinois by 13 November 1848. JOHANN MÜLLER (MUELLER) died at his home in McHenry, McHenry County, Illinois on 21 January 1908. Burial 24 January 1908 at St. Mary's Catholic Cemetery in McHenry:
https://www. findagrave. com/memorial/71757607/john-mueller

Obituary, McHenry Plaindealer, 30 January 1908, Front page.

JOHANN MUELLER & SUSANNA GOEDERT-SCHMITT

Early Records of St. Joseph's Catholic Church
Wilmette, Cook County, Illinois:
Johann MÜLLER & Susanna SCHMITT
Married 5 March 1849
Witnesses: Wilhelm KLEIN & Jacob SCHMITT

Susanna and Johann celebrated their Golden Anniversary in May 1899. See: McHenry Plaindealer, 19 May 1899, Front page.

SUSANNA & JOHANN were the parents of the following children, birth and baptism of their first two children born in Johnsburg, were recorded at St. Joseph's Catholic Church in Wilmette, Cook County, Illinois. Their remaining 14 children, who were also born in Johnsburg, were recorded at St. John the Baptist Catholic Church in Johnsburg:

8. i. PETER MUELLER (1850-1858)
9. ii. GERTRUD MUELLER (1851-1855)
10. iii. WILHELM MUELLER (1852-1928)
11. iv. NICOLAUS MUELLER (1854-1855)
12. v. MARIA K. MUELLER (MILLER) LENZEN (1855-1935)
13. vi. JOHANN WILHELM MUELLER (MILLER) (1857-1935)
14. vii. MARIA MUELLER (1858-1896)
15. viii. NIKOLAUS MUELLER (1859-1883)
16. ix. PETER HENRY MUELLER (MILLER) (1861-1912)
17. x. ANNA MUELLER (1863-1870)
18. xi. SUSANNA MUELLER (1865-1865)
19. xii. ANNA M. "EMMA" MUELLER KENNEBECK (1867-1932)
20. xiii. MAGDALENA MUELLER (1871-1871)
21. xiv. ELIZABETH "LIZZIE" MUELLER (1872-1919)
22. xv. MARIA MUELLER (1872-1881)
23. xvi. JOSEPHINA MUELLER MAYER (1873-1956)

JOHANN & SUSANNA (SCHMITT) MUELLER FAMILY

(IMAGE AT BOTTOM OF FACING PAGE:)

JOHANN & SUSANNA (SCHMITT) MUELLER FAMILY; CIRCA 1886; JOHN MUELLER & SUSANNA NEE GOEDERT-SCHMITT WERE THE PARENTS OF 16 KNOWN CHILDREN. IN THIS PHOTO ARE SOME OF THEIR CHILDREN WHO SURVIVED TO ADULTHOOD, AS A SON APPEARS TO BE MISSING FROM THE PHOTO, POSSIBLY SON NIKOLAUS (1859-1883).
FRONT ROW, L TO R: ELIZABETH "LIZZIE" MUELLER (SHE NEVER MARRIED), FATHER JOHANN MUELLER, MOTHER SUSANNA MUELLER NEE GOEDERT-SCHMITT, JOSEPHINE MUELLER (JOSEPH MEYER/MAYER).
BACK ROW, L TO R: ANNA MARIA "EMMA" MUELLER (2ND WIFE OF JOHN HENRY KENNEBECK), JOHN W. (MARGARET LENZEN), PETER HENRY (SUSAN PENNEY), WILLIAM (EMMA HUEMANN), MARY K (JOHANN LENZEN), AND MARIA (WHO NEVER MARRIED).

Grandchildren (Bold Black)
Great-grandchildren (Fuchsia)
2x Great-grandchildren (Teal)

8. PETER MUELLER Born on 26 February 1850 in Johnsburg, McHenry County, Illinois. Peter died in Johnsburg on 25 June 1858. Burial at St. John the Baptist Cemetery in Johnsburg: https://www.findagrave.com/memorial/80305022/peter-mueller

9. GERTRUD MUELLER Born on 8 July 1851 in Johnsburg, McHenry County, Illinois. Gertrud died in Johnsburg on 4 May 1855. Burial at St. John the Baptist Cemetery in Johnsburg: https://www.findagrave.com/memorial/80304520/gertrud-mueller

10. **WILHELM (WILLIAM) MUELLER** Born on 19 August 1852 in Johnsburg, McHenry County, Illinois. William died in Adams, Mower County, Minnesota on 4 June 1928. Burial at Sacred Heart Cemetery in Adams:
https://www.findagrave.com/memorial/38952977/william-mueller

On 19 November 1878, WILLIAM MÜLLER married ANNA MARIA (MARY) HUEMANN (HUMANN), daughter of MATHIAS HUEMANN (1820-1882) & CHRISTINA SCHNEIDER (1824-1901), at Visitation Catholic Church in Stacyville, Mitchell County, Iowa. MARY HUEMANN was born on 1 January 1858 in Johnsburg (named after the village in McHenry County, Illinois), Mower County, Minnesota. Mary died on 16 March 1927 in Adams, Mower County, Minnesota. Burial at Sacred Heart Cemetery in Adams:
https://www.findagrave.com/memorial/38953031/anna-maria-mueller

WILLIAM MUELLER & MARY HUEMANN

The following very interesting letter from William Mueller appeared in the McHenry Plaindealer. William sent the letter to the editor of the Plaindealer. He had the McHenry (Illinois) newspaper sent to him while he resided in Minnesota.

McHenry Plaindealer, 7 July 1926, Column 7:
Letter received from William Mueller of Adams, Mower County, Minnesota, 28 June 1926:

> *"Dear Editor:*
> *As my subscription has run out will again renew. We had a very cold and wet spring up here, but it is getting warmer now. Today it is 90 in the shade with clear sky and south wind. Corn is very backward, at least three weeks. Say editor, the history of Johnsburg just suited me. I was born in 1852. Left the county fifty three years ago for the then wild west, crossing the Mississippi River at McGregor on a ferry boat when but a boy. Things have changed since. I am bald headed, have seven children living, thirty-four grandchildren and am now a widower and a lonesome old man. The first child baptized at Johnsburg, was my uncle, now living at Jamestown, North Dakota.*
> *Yours Truly, Wm Mueller."*
>
> **NOTE:** The "first child baptized" refers to William's maternal uncle, Nicholas Schmitt, son of Jacob Schmitt a founder of Johnsburg, and Anna Goedert.

WILLIAM & MARY were the parents of:
- 55. i. ANNA MUELLER (1879-1897)
- 56. ii. NICHOLAS MUELLER (1881-1967)
- 57. iii. JOSEPHINE MUELLER KLAPPERICH (1882-1977)
- 58. iv. MARY MUELLER BLAKE (1884-1972)
- 59. v. WILLIAM MUELLER (1887-1892)
- 60. vi. CHRISTINA MUELLER (1889-1892)
- 61. vii. CHRISTINA MUELLER KLAPPERICH (1891-1982)
- 62. viii. JOHN JOSEPH G. MUELLER (1893-1971)
- 63. ix. MARGARETHA MUELLER (1895-1897)

64. x.   ELIZABETH MUELLER SCHAEFER
         (1897-1965)
65. xi. HELENA MUELLER MICHELS
         (1900-1978)

55. ANNA MUELLER Born on 24 August 1879 in Stacyville, Mitchell County, Iowa. Anna died on 7 June 1897 in Stacyville. Burial 9 June 1897 at Visitation Cemetery in Stacyville:
https://www.findagrave.com/memorial/71166374/anna-mueller

56. NICHOLAS MUELLER Born on 8 March 1881 in Stacyville, Mitchell County, Iowa. Nicholas died in Riceville, Mitchell County, Iowa on 25 December 1967. Burial at Calvary Cemetery in Riceville:
https://www.findagrave.com/memorial/27455015/nicholas-mueller

On 15 September 1904, NICHOLAS MUELLER married RACHEL CRAIG, the adopted daughter of MATHIAS GOERGEN (1840-1921) & ELIZABETH nee GOERGEN (1842-1936), at Sacred Heart Catholic Church in Meyer, Mitchell County, Iowa. RACHEL CRAIG-GOERGEN was born on 18 March 1886 in New York City, New York. RACHEL CRAIG was an orphan adopted by the GOERGEN family, who lived near Bailey, Mitchell County, Iowa. MATHIAS GOERGEN and ELIZABETH nee GOERGEN came from Steinberg, Dist. Vogtland, Saxony, Prussia to America about 1881 and settled first in Milwaukee, Milwaukee County, Wisconsin. They then moved on to Bailey, Mitchell County, Iowa. Rachel died in Riceville, Mitchell County, Iowa on 18 February 1968. Burial at Calvary Cemetery in Riceville. There is a family photo on her memorial, taken in 1954, contributed by Mr. John Mueller:
https://www.findagrave.com/memorial/27455047/rachel-mueller

NOTE: Records show that Rachel was not born in Iowa. Rachel was left at the "New York Foundling Hospital", 1175 3rd Avenue, New York City, at the age of 6 days. She was baptized Rachel CRAIG at "St. Vincent Ferrerer Catholic Church" on 24 March 1886, by Father Slinger. At about the age of 3 years, Rachel was placed aboard a west bound orphan train with a note that contained her given name and the name of the GOERGEN family, and a destination address of Adams, Iowa. Her birth parents names were not found in the foundling home documents". Source: From Langenfeld to Johnsburg published in 2008 by a family descendant and family researcher, Teryl "Terry" Miller (1937-2020).

NICHOLAS & RACHEL were the parents of the following children (their photos are on their memorials on findagrave.com):

i. ARNOLD MATHIAS MUELLER (1905-2005)
ii. ROSINA MUELLER DURBEN (1907-1989)
iii. ESTHER MARIE MUELLER HARTOGH (1909-2002)
iv. AGNES ELIZABETH MUELLER BEES (1911-1994)
v. CARL MUELLER (1914-1973) WW II Veteran, Corporal in U. S. Army
vi. FRANCIS XAVIER MUELLER (1916-1979) WW II Veteran, U. S. Army
vii. RAYMOND "PETE" MUELLER (1918-1977) WW II Veteran, PFC in U. S. Army
viii. MARTHA MUELLER DUEBNER (1921-2003)
ix. PAUL JOSEPH MUELLER (1924-2023) WW II Veteran, U. S. Army
x. WILLIAM JOSEPH MUELLER (1926-2011)
xi. REYNOLD JOSEPH "BUTCH" MUELLER (1929-2013)

57. JOSEPHINE MUELLER Born on 15 September 1882 in Stacyville, Mitchell County, Iowa. Josephine died in Meyer,

Mitchell County, Iowa on 2 May 1977. Burial at Sacred Heart Cemetery in Meyer:
https://www.findagrave.com/memorial/38583109/josephine-klapperich

On 19 October 1905, JOSEPHINE MUELLER married MATHIAS KLAPPERICH, son of MICHAEL KLAPPERICH (1850-1934) & BARBARA MARY BELL (1861-1937), at Sacred Heart Catholic Church in Meyer, Mitchell County, Iowa. MATHIAS KLAPPERICH was born on 18 September 1882 in Stacyville, Mitchell County, Iowa. Mathias died in Meyer, Mitchell County, Iowa on 10 July 1957. Burial at Sacred Heart Cemetery in Meyer:
https://www.findagrave.com/memorial/38583151/mathias-klapperich

JOSEPHINE & MATHIAS were the parents of:
i. MARTHA MARIA KLAPPERICH BREISTER (1906-1996)
i. ARTHUR ANTON KLAPPERICH (1907-1996)
iii. ANNA MARIA "EMMA" KLAPPERICH STEFFEN (1909-1996)
https://www.findagrave.com/memorial/108339375/anna-marie-steffen
iv. EDWARD KLAPPERICH (1916-1994)

58. **MARY MUELLER** Born on 8 May 1884 in Meyer, Mitchell County, Iowa. Mary died in Stacyville, Mitchell County, Iowa on 9 January 1972. Burial at Visitation Cemetery in Stacyville:
https://www.findagrave.com/memorial/37193196/mary-blake

On 11 February 1904, MARY MUELLER married JOSEPH BLAKE, son of PHILLIP BLAKE (1838-1921) & JUSTINA AGUSTA "GUSTINA" SMITH (1847-1905), at Sacred Heart

Catholic Church in Meyer, Mitchell County, Iowa. JOSEPH BLAKE was born on 2 October 1881 in Stacyville, Mitchell County, Iowa. Joseph died in Stacyville on 28 December 1963. Burial at Visitation Cemetery in Stacyville:
https://www.findagrave.com/memorial/37193263/joseph-blake

MARY & JOSEPH were the parents of:
i.   ERNEST F. BLAKE (1904-1980)
ii. LEONA BLAKE ROBINSON (1908-1996)
iii. EDWIN H. BLAKE (1912-1993)
iv. BERTHA KATHERINE BLAKE (1914-1930)
v.   OLIVE HELEN BLAKE KOENIGS (1919-2001)
vi. G. FRANK (FRANK G.) BLAKE (1923-2012)

59. WILLIAM MUELLER Born on 21 May 1887 in Stacyville, Mitchell County, Iowa. William died on 15 June 1892 in Stacyville. Burial at Visitation Cemetery in Stacyville:
https://www.findagrave.com/memorial/71166240/william-mueller

60. CHRISTINA MUELLER Born on 3 December 1889 in Stacyville, Mitchell County, Iowa. Christina died on 11 January 1892 in Stacyville. Burial at Visitation Cemetery in Stacyville.

61. CHRISTINA MUELLER Born on 23 December 1891 in Stacyville, Mitchell County, Iowa. Christina died in Adams, Mower County, Minnesota on 4 November 1982. Burial at Sacred Heart Cemetery in Adams:
https://www.findagrave.com/memorial/34188663/christina-klapperich

On 14 May 1912, CHRISTINA MUELLER married STEPHAN MICHAEL KLAPPERICH, son of MICHAEL KLAPPERICH (1850-1934) & BARBARA BELL (1861-1937), at Sacred Heart Catholic Church in Meyer, Mitchell County, Iowa. STEPHAN KLAPPERICH was born on 21 August 1887 in Meyer, Mitchell

County, Iowa. Stephan died in Adams, Mower County, Minnesota on 4 December 1968. Burial at Sacred Heart Cemetery in Adams. In a MICHAEL KLAPPERICH family photo, circa 1910, Stephan is in the back row on the memorial: https://www.findagrave.com/memorial/34188654/stephan-m-klapperich

CHRISTINA & STEPHAN were parents of:
i. HERMAN JOSEPH KLAPPERICH (1922-1998) WW II Veteran, U. S. Navy:
https://www.findagrave.com/memorial/25262665/herman_joseph_klapperich
ii. ROBERT JOHN KLAPPERICH (1925-1943):
https://www.findagrave.com/memorial/34188642/robert_j_klapperich
iii. Sr. BARBARA ANN KLAPPERICH (1929-1999):
https://www.findagrave.com/memorial/127553737/barbara_ann_klapperich
iv. ISABELLA HELEN KLAPPERICH MORSE (1931-2023):
https://www.findagrave.com/memorial/259818719/isabella_helen_morse
v. NICHOLAS KLAPPERICH (1934-2011):
https://www.findagrave.com/memorial/69942812/nicholas_klapperich

62. JOHN JOSEPH MUELLER Born on 28/29 August 1893 in Little Cedar, Mitchell County, Iowa. John died in Stacyville, Mitchell County, Iowa on 25 May 1971. Burial at Visitation Cemetery in Stacyville. Obituary is on his memorial page: https://www.findagrave.com/memorial/38523242/john-joseph-mueller

On 26 January 1916, JOHN MUELLER married ELIZABETH BERTHA THOME, daughter of JOHN THOME (1862-1946) & SARAH MARY STEIGER (1872-1931), at Sacred Heart Catholic

Church in Meyer, Mitchell County, Iowa. ELIZABETH THOME was born on 26 September 1895 in Stacyville, Mitchell County, Iowa. Elizabeth died in Stacyville on 25 May 1992. Burial at Visitation Cemetery in Stacyville. Obituary is on her memorial page:
https://www.findagrave.com/memorial/38523287/elizabeth-bertha-mueller

John Joseph Mueller & Elizabeth Thome

JOHN & ELIZABETH were the parents of the following children. Their photos and some obituaries are on their memorial page on findagrave.com:

i. CYRILLA ELIZABETH MUELLER ROCKERS (1916-2015)

ii. VIOLA SARAH MUELLER (1918-1928)
iii. EVELYN HELEN MUELLER BRUMM (1919-2003)
iv. EMIL FREDERICH MUELLER (1921-2012) WW II Veteran: https://www.findagrave.com/memorial/88712801/emil_fredrick_mueller
v. JOHN MUELLER (1923-1923)
vi. ELMER JOSEPH MUELLER (1925- Living 24 February 2021)
vii. MAXINE MUELLER HALBACH (1927- Living 24 February 2021)
viii. IRENE VIOLA MUELLER HEMANN (1928-2021): https://www.findagrave.com/memorial/58455097/irene_viola_hemann
ix. MARVIN JOSEPH MUELLER (1930- before 15 April 2012)
x. DELPHIN CARL MUELLER (1932- Living 24 February 2021)
xi. ANITA LEONA MUELLER ADAMS (1934- Living 24 February 2021)
xii. LAVERN STEPHEN MUELLER (1937-2019) Veteran, U. S. Army: https://www.findagrave.com/memorial/197553049/lavern_steven_mueller
xiii. MARY ANN MUELLER MULLENBACH (b. After 1940-Living 24 February 2021)

63. **MARGARETHA MUELLER** Born on 3 August 1895 in Stacyville, Mitchell County, Iowa. Margaretha died on 25 June

1897 in Stacyville. Burial at Visitation Cemetery in Stacyville:
https://www.findagrave.com/memorial/71166168/margratha-mueller

64. ELIZABETH MUELLER Born on 24 October 1897 in Stacyville, Mitchell County, Iowa. Elizabeth died in Adams, Mower County, Minnesota on 14 September 1965. Burial at Sacred Heart Cemetery in Adams:
https://www.findagrave.com/memorial/34216641/elizabeth-a-schaefer

On 28 November 1917, ELIZABETH MUELLER married JOSEPH SYLVESTER SCHAEFER, son of MATHIAS SCHAEFER (1849-1915) & SUSANNA SCHAFF (1859-1935), in Adams, Mower County, Minnesota. JOSEPH SCHAEFER was born on 28 February 1889 in Adams, Mower County, Minnesota. Joseph died in Adams on 5 April 1983. Burial at Sacred Heart Cemetery in Adams:
https://www.findagrave.com/memorial/34216621/joseph-s-schaefer

JOSEPH SCHAEFER & ELIZABETH MUELLER

ELIZABETH & JOSEPH were the parents of the following children. Their photos and obituaries are on their memorials on findagrave.com.

i. PAUL MATHIAS SCHAEFER (1918-1992):
   https://www.findagrave.com/memorial/paul_mathias_schaefer
ii. FLORENCE EMELINE SCHAEFER SCHMITZ (1919-2018):
   https://www.findagrave.com/memorial/189529049/florence_emily_schmitz
iii. VERNON JOSEPH SCHAEFER (1922-1988) WW II Veteran, U. S. Army:
   https://www.findagrave.com/memorial/208787738/vernon_joseph_schaefer
iv. FREDERICK WILLIAM SCHAEFER (1923-2010) WW II Veteran, Tech 3 U. S. Army:
   https://www.findagrave.com/memorial/54274546/frederick_william_schaefer
v. HERBERT ALPHONSE SCHAEFER (1925-2011) WW II Veteran, U. S. Army:
   https://www.findagrave.com/memorial/68359617/herbert_alphonse_schaefer
vi. BENNO JOSEPH SCHAEFER (1928-2006) Veteran, U. S. Navy:
   https://www.findagrave.com/memorial/13628772/benno_joseph_schaefer
vii. MARCELLA ELIZABETH SCHAEFER PERRIN (1930-2011):
   https://www.findagrave.com/memorial/78018363/marcella_elizabeth_perrin
viii. NORBERT ERNEST SCHAEFER (1932-2018) Korean War Veteran, U. S. Army:
   https://www.findagrave.com/memorial/197466288/norbert_ernest_schaefer
ix. RITA SCHAEFER SHEEDY
   (1934- Living 20 May 2021)

x.   **CONRAD J. SCHAEFER**
     (1937- Living 20 May 2021)
xi. **ROGER T. SCHAEFER (1939-2021)**
     Veteran, U. S. Army:
     https://www.findagrave.com/memorial/243992724/roger_thomas_schaefer
xii. **ELIZABETH MARGARET "BETTE" SCHAEFER SMITH (1941-2021):**
     https://www.findagrave.com/memorial/229956166/elizabeth_margaret_smith
     Obituary:
     https://www.legacy.com/us/obituaries/daily-southtown/name/elizabeth-smith-obituary?id=11520505

65. HELENA MUELLER Born on 26 April 1900 in Liberty Township, Mitchell County, Iowa. Helena died in Stacyville, Mitchell County, Iowa on 10 October 1978. Burial at Visitation Cemetery in Stacyville:
https://www.findagrave.com/memorial/39178844/helen-l-michels

On 23 October 1919, HELENA MUELLER married JOSEPH FLORIAN MICHELS, son of PETER MICHELS (1862-1937) & MARGARETHA SCHMITT (1866-1937), at Visitation Catholic Church in Stacyville, Mitchell County, Iowa. JOSEPH FLORIAN MICHELS was born on 4 June 1898 in Stacyville, Mitchell County, Iowa. Joseph died in Stacyville on 28 September 1952. Burial at Visitation Cemetery in Stacyville:
https://www.findagrave.com/memorial/39168752/joseph-florian-michels

JOSEPH MICHELS & HELENA MUELLER

HELENA & JOSEPH were the parents of the following known children. Photos and some obituaries are on their memorial page:

i. WILMER PETER "BUD" MICHELS (1920-2006): https://www.findagrave.com/memorial/14971923/wilmer_peter_michels
ii. ETHEL CATHERINE MICHELS BISSEN (1921-2018): https://www.postbulletin.com/obituaries/ethel-c-bissen-stewartville
iii. PATRICIA MICHELS MURDOCK (1927- bef 18 September 2008)
iv. RUTH MARIE MICHELS OLSON (1929- Living 28 October 2019)
v. JOSEPH LEON "PETE" MICHELS (1932-2019) Veteran, U. S. Army: https://www.findagrave.com/memorial/242921562/joseph_leon_michels

https://www. legacy. com/us/obituaries/globegazette/name/joseph-michels-obituary?id=32861411

vi. JOHN NICHOLAS "JACK" MICHELS (1935-2008) Veteran, U. S. Navy:
https://www. findagrave. com/memorial/39178999/john_nicholas_michels

vii. HAZEL LEONA MICHELS HEIMER (1937-2017):
https://www. findagrave. com/memorial/177423416/hazel_leona_heimer

11. **NICOLAUS MUELLER** Born on 9 August 1854 in Johnsburg, McHenry County, Illinois. Nicolaus died in Johnsburg on 3 October 1855. Burial at St. John the Baptist Cemetery in Johnsburg:
https://www. findagrave. com/memorial/80305005/nicolaus-mueller

12. **MARIA KATHARINA (MARY) MUELLER** Born on 25 November 1855 in Johnsburg, McHenry County, Illinois. Mary died in Wauconda, Lake County, Illinois on 23 March 1935. Burial 26 March 1935 at St. Peter's Cemetery in Volo, Lake County, Illinois:
https://www. findagrave. com/memorial/35693752/mary-katherine-lenzen

On 30 September 1875, MARIA KATHARINA (MARY) MUELLER married JOHANN (JOHN) LENZEN, son of MICHAEL JOHN LENZEN (1825-1898) & ANNA MARIA ADOLPHI (1829-1909), at St. John the Baptist Catholic Church in Johnsburg, McHenry County, Illinois. JOHANN LENZEN was born on 15 December 1850 in Heyroth, Dist. of Vulkaneifel, Rhineland, Prussia. John died in Wauconda, Lake County, Illinois on 8 November 1920. Burial at St. Peter's Cemetery in Volo, Lake County, Illinois:
https://www. findagrave. com/memorial/19508840/john-lenzen

John Lenzen & Mary Mueller

MARY & JOHN were the parents of:
66. i. MARIA M. "MARY" LENZEN DUTZLER (1876-1966)
67. ii. SUSANNA KATHERINE LENZEN TEKAMPE (1877-1958)
68. iii. JOHANN JOSEPH LENZEN (1878-1965)
69. iv. MARGARETHA EVA "MARGARET" LENZEN TEKAMPE (1880-1930)
70. v. MICHAEL GEORGE LENZEN (1882-1963)
71. vi. WILLIAM EDWARD LENZEN (1883-1955)
72. vii. BERNARD ALBERT LENZEN (1885-1965)
73. viii. ANNA CECELIA LENZEN BEHM (1887-1963)
74. ix. LEONARD HENRY LENZEN (1890-1918) WW I, Pvt in U. S. Army
75. x. MARIA "CATHARINE" B. LENZEN BEHM (1892-1949)
76. xi. JOSEPH FRANK LENZEN (1895-1977)

66. MARIA LENZEN Born on 4 August 1876 in Burton Township, McHenry County, Illinois. Maria died in Hainesville, Lake County, Illinois on 12 August 1966. Burial at St. Mary Catholic Cemetery, Fremont Township, Lake County, Illinois:
https://www.findagrave.com/memorial/53625395/mary-m_-dutzler

On 6 October 1898, MARIA LENZEN married VITUS F. DUTZLER, son of MICHAEL DUTZLER (abt 1827-1886) & MARIA ALT (abt 1835-1916) at St. Mary's Catholic Church in Fremont Township, Lake County, Illinois. VITUS DUTZLER was born on 31 December 1867 (or 1 January 1869: his birth date as it is recorded on his Death Record), in Perrysburg, Wood County, Ohio. VITUS DUTZLER died when struck by an automobile in Hainesville, Lake County, Illinois on 30 December 1936. Burial at St. Mary Catholic Cemetery in Fremont Center, Lake County, Illinois:
https://www.findagrave.com/memorial/53625209/vitus-f_-dutzler

MARIA & VITUS were the parents of:
  i. CECILIA DUTZLER OBENAUF (1900-2001)
  ii. JOHN JOSEPH DUTZLER (1902-1985)
  iii. CLARA SUSANNE DUTZLER BAIER (1903-1984)
  iv. ALBERT JOHN DUTZLER (1905-1988)
  v. JOSEPH EDWARD DUTZLER (1907-1992)
  vi. JULIA A. DUTZLER (1910-1997)
  vii. LEONARD HENRY DUTZLER (1913-1980)

67. SUSANNA KATHERINE LENZEN Born on 12 November 1877 in Burton Township, McHenry County, Illinois. Susanna died in Libertyville, Lake County, Illinois on 20 April 1958. Burial at St. Mary Catholic Cemetery in Fremont Center:
https://www.findagrave.com/memorial/55119832/susanna-katherine-tekampe

On 21 June 1905, SUSANNA LENZEN married JOHN MICHAEL TEKAMPE, son of WILLIAM TEKAMPE (1836-1911)

& MARGARETHA FIRNBACH (1840-1910), at St. Mary Catholic Church in Fremont Center, Lake County, Illinois. JOHN MICHAEL TEKAMPE was born on 31 October 1876 in Fremont Center, Lake County, Illinois. He died in Fremont Center on 14 April 1943. Burial at St. Mary Catholic Cemetery in Fremont Center:

https://www.findagrave.com/memorial/55119616/john-michael-tekampe

SUSANNA & JOHN were the parents of the following children, including two sets of twins: twin sisters Laura & Ludwina; and twin brothers, Oscar & Ralph:

i. LAURA MARGARET TEKAMPE HERTEL (1906-1997)
ii. LUDWINA M. TEKAMPE WINTER (1906-1987)
iii. ROSINA ANNA TEKAMPE WEIDNER (1908-1988)
iv. OSCAR J. TEKAMPE (1911-1926)
v. RALPH MICHAEL TEKAMPE (1911-1992)
vi. ANDREW ISIDORE TEKAMPE (1914-2007)

68. JOHN JOSEPH LENZEN Born on 17 November 1878 in Burton Township, McHenry County, Illinois. John died in Round Lake, Lake County, Illinois on 17 November 1965. Burial at St. Mary Catholic Cemetery in Fremont Center, Lake County, Illinois:

https://www.findagrave.com/memorial/19508985/john-joseph-lenzen

On 28 February 1905, JOHN LENZEN married 1. MARTHA FRANCES WAGNER, daughter of JOHN WAGNER (1847-1934) & CAROLINA MUSSER (1849-1918), at St. Mary Catholic Church in Fremont Center, Lake County, Illinois. MARTHA FRANCES WAGNER was born on 26 February 1886 in Fremont Center. Martha died on 22 April 1908 in Fremont Center. Burial at St. Mary Catholic Cemetery in Fremont Center:

https://www.findagrave.com/memorial/24460086/martha-a_-lenzen

JOHN & 1. MARTHA WAGNER were the parents of one child:
i.   ALBERT BERNARD LENZEN (1906-1992):
https://www.findagrave.com/memorial/121105857/albert_b_lenzen

On 6 September 1911, JOHN LENZEN married 2. MARY ELIZABETH WAGNER, daughter of MARTIN WAGNER (1861-1950) & ANNA MARGARET SPOERL (1861-1948), at St. Mary Catholic Church in Fremont Center, Lake County, Illinois. MARY ELIZABETH WAGNER was born on 22 August 1888 in Fremont Center, Lake County, Illinois. Mary died in Round Lake, Lake County, Illinois on 13 December 1949. Burial at St. Mary Catholic Cemetery in Fremont Center, Lake County, Illinois: https://www.findagrave.com/memorial/24461042/mary-elizabeth-lenzen

JOHN & 2. MARY WAGNER were the parents of:
i.   EDWARD MICHAEL LENZEN (1912-1987) WW II Veteran, U. S. Army: https://www.findagrave.com/memorial/19508711/edward_michael_lenzen
ii. FREDERICK RICHARD LENZEN (1913-1991)
iii. LEO JOHN LENZEN (1914-1986)
iv. MARTIN ANTHONY LENZEN (1916-1994)
v.   MARCELLA A. LENZEN KOEHLER (1920-1999)
vi. THERESA E. LENZEN DIETZ (1928-2018)

69. MARGARET EVA LENZEN Born on 23 July 1880 in Burton Township, McHenry County, Illinois. Margaret died in Fremont Center, Lake County, Illinois on 6 August 1930. Burial at St. Mary Catholic Cemetery in Fremont Center:
https://www.findagrave.com/memorial/53626178/margaret-eva-tekampe

On 6 November 1906, MARGARET LENZEN married JOSEPH FRANCIS TEKAMPE, son of WILLIAM TEKAMPE (1836-1911)

& MARGARETHA FIRNBACH (1840-1910), at St. Mary Catholic Church in Fremont Center, Lake County, Illinois. JOSEPH TEKAMPE was born on 4 December 1878 in Fremont Center, Lake County, Illinois. Joseph died in Fremont Center on 20 September 1969. Burial at St. Mary Catholic Cemetery in Fremont Center: https://www.findagrave.com/memorial/53625842/joseph-francis-tekampe

JOSEPH TEKAMPE & MARGARET LENZEN

MARGARET & JOSEPH were the parents of the following children, including two sets of twins. All children lived to adulthood. Twin Margaret Mary Tekampe Paddock died age 101 years, a Centenarian.

i. REGINA CATHERINE TEKAMPE WEIDNER (1908-1997) Twin of CHRISTINA.

ii. CHRISTINA MARGARET TEKAMPE LEFFELMAN (1908-1993) Twin of REGINA.
iii. LEO JOHN TEKAMPE (1911-1995)

   Note: Wedding photo on his memorial page:
   https://www.findagrave.com/memorial/114822409/leo-john-tekampe

iv. MARTHA CATHERINE TEKAMPE ROSSDUETCHER (1913-2008)
v. JOSEPH VITUS TEKAMPE (1916-1978) Twin of MARGARET.

   Note: Wedding photo appears on his memorial page:
   https://www.findagrave.com/memorial/158062891/joseph_vitus_tekampe

vi. MARGARET MARY TEKAMPE PADDOCK (1916-2017) Twin of JOSEPH.

   Note: Wedding photo on her memorial page, also her 101st birthday celebration photo, Amazing!:
   https://www.findagrave.com/memorial/69006288/margaret_mary_paddock

MARGARET MARY TEKAMPE PADDOCK

70. MICHAEL GEORGE LENZEN Born on 21 January 1882 in Burton Township, McHenry County, Illinois. Michael died in

McHenry, McHenry County, Illinois on 9 March 1963. Burial at St. Mary's Catholic Cemetery in McHenry:
https://www.findagrave.com/memorial/21299810/michael-george-lenzen

On 19 May 1915, MICHAEL GEORGE LENZEN married EVA THERESA MILLER, daughter of MATHIAS MILLER (1864-1892) & LUCY HERBES (1870-1958), at St. Peter's Catholic Church in Volo, Lake County, Illinois. EVA MILLER was born on 19 May 1889 in Johnsburg, McHenry County, Illinois. Eva died in McHenry, McHenry County, Illinois on 21 April 1969. Burial at St. Mary's Catholic Cemetery in McHenry:
https://www.findagrave.com/memorial/21299830/eva-lenzen

MICHAEL GEORGE & EVA were the parents of:

i. ROMAN JOHN LENZEN (1916-1997)
   WW II Veteran, SM2 U. S. Navy:
   https://www.findagrave.com/memorial/88417496/roman_john_lenzen

ii. EUGENE VIANNEY "JEAN" LENZEN (1919-1986):
    https://www.findagrave.com/memorial/243032415/jean_vianney_lenzen

iii. JEROME WILLIAM LENZEN
     (1921-2001) WW II Veteran,
     41st Armored Army Signal Corps:
     https://www.findagrave.com/memorial/7232015/jerome_lenzen

iv. HERMAN JOSEPH LENZEN
    (1923-2004) WW II Veteran, PFC U. S. Army:
    https://www.findagrave.com/memorial/32890648/herman_joseph_lenzen

v. PHYLISS LENZEN NEARGARDER (1925-2004)

vi. ANTOINETTE LENZEN REIMERS (1926-2019)

vii. FRANCES H. LENZEN RILEY (1928-2018)
viii. INFANT LENZEN

71. WILLIAM EDWARD LENZEN Born on 17 October 1883 in Burton Township, McHenry County, Illinois. William died in Grayslake, Lake County, Illinois on 30 December 1955. Burial at St. Joseph Catholic Cemetery in Round Lake, Lake County, Illinois:
https://www.findagrave.com/memorial/30702944/william-edward-lenzen

Between 1920 and the 1930 census, WILLIAM EDWARD LENZEN married CAROLINE MARIE KEIL, daughter of HUBERT KEIL (1833-1897) & CAROLINE FREUND (1850-?). CAROLINE MARIE KEIL was born on 14 October 1880 in Wheeling, Cook County, Illinois. Caroline died in Waukegan, Lake County, Illinois on 21 April 1960. Burial at St. Joseph Catholic Cemetery in Round Lake, Lake County, Illinois:
https://www.findagrave.com/memorial/182954616/caroline-marie-lenzen

WILLIAM & CAROLINE had no known children.

72. BERNARD ALBERT LENZEN Born on 22 June 1885 in Volo, Lake County, Illinois. Bernard died in Grayslake, Lake County, Illinois on 3 February 1965. Burial at St. Mary Catholic Cemetery in Fremont Center, Lake County, Illinois:
https://www.findagrave.com/memorial/28891280/bernard-albert-lenzen

On 19 November 1913, BERNARD LENZEN married ELIZABETH MARGARET STOFFEL, daughter of JOSEPH M. STOFFEL (1862-1915) & MARIA GERTRUDE ROSING

(1866-1963), at St. Mary Catholic Church in Fremont Center, Lake County, Illinois. ELIZABETH MARGARET STOFFEL was born on 14 October 1891 in Lyons, Burt County, Nebraska. Elizabeth died in Libertyville, Lake County, Illinois on 26 February 1979. Burial at St. Mary Catholic Cemetery in Fremont Center, Lake County, Illinois:
https://www.findagrave.com/memorial/28891372/elizabeth-margaret-lenzen

Bernard and Elizabeth celebrated their Golden Anniversary in November 1963.

BERNARD & ELIZABETH were the parents of:
i. MARY AGNES CLARE LENZEN (1914-2009)
   Note: Baptized Mary Gertrude:
   https://www.findagrave.com/memorial/140972652/m_agnes_clare_lenzen
ii. CATHERINE LENZEN AUGENBAUGH (1916-1990)
iii. ROSE GERTRUDE LENZEN KLABUNDE (1917-2016):
   https://www.findagrave.com/memorial/161702950/rose_g_klabunde
iv. JOSEPHINE CATHERINE LENZEN (1919-2009):
   https://www.findagrave.com/memorial/43549935/josephine_c_lenzen
v. LORETTA MARY LENZEN MANKE (1921-1987):
   https://www.findagrave.com/memorial/25912574/loretta_mary_manke
vi. CECILIA CATHERINE LENZEN DIEDRICH (1923-2007):
   https://www.findagrave.com/memorial/23729604/cecilia_catherina_diedrich
vii. CLARA E. LENZEN TONYAN (1924-Living 27 January 2022)
viii. BERNARD J. LENZEN (1925-Living 8 January 2023)

ix. JOSEPH WILLIAM LENZEN (1927-2019):
https://www.findagrave.com/memorial/203916225/joseph_william_lenzen
x. FLORENCE MARY LENZEN WEIDNER (1929-2022):
https://www.legacy.com/us/obituaries/nwherald/name/florence-weidner-obituary?id=32596981
xi. CLARENCE I. (MIDGE) LENZEN (1932-2018) Veteran, U. S. Marine Corps:
https://www.findagrave.com/memorial/194917772/larence_i_lenzen
xii. JOHN B. LENZEN (1934- 2018):
https://www.findagrave.com/memorial/189449614/john_b_lenzen

73. ANNA CECELIA LENZEN Born on 6 August 1887 in Volo, Lake County, Illinois. Anna died in Fremont Center, Lake County, Illinois on 3 September 1963. Burial at St. Mary Catholic Cemetery in Fremont Center:
https://www.findagrave.com/memorial/19508585/anna-cecelia-behm

On 5 October 1911, ANNA CECELIA LENZEN married ISIDOR MICHAEL BEHM, son of ADAM BEHM (1851-1929) & MARIA HERTEL (1856-1945), at St. Mary Catholic Church in Fremont Center, Lake County, Illinois. ISIDOR MICHAEL BEHM was born on 27 May 1882 in Fremont Center, Lake County, Illinois. Isidor died in Libertyville, Lake County, Illinois on 14 December 1973. Burial at St. Mary Catholic Cemetery in Fremont Center, Lake County, Illinois:
https://www.findagrave.com/memorial/19363536/isidor-michael-behm

ANNA & ISIDOR were the parents of:
i. GEORGE MARCUS BEHM (1912-1993):
https://www.findagrave.com/memorial/19363459/george_marcus_behm

ii. MARTIN ALBERT BEHM (1913-2003):
https://www.findagrave.com/memorial/20039481/martin_albert_behm
iii. LUCILLE MARY BEHM WEIDNER (1915-2002):
https://www.findagrave.com/memorial/22102590/lucille_mary_weidner
iv. ANTHONY J. BEHM (1918-1993):
https://www.findagrave.com/memorial/19363291/anthony_j_behm
v. ROBERT JOSEPH BEHM (1920-1981):
https://www.findagrave.com/memorial/20061889/robert_joseph_behm
vi. EVELYN S. BEHM CHAMBERLIN (1922-2016):
https://www.findagrave.com/memorial/159607070/evelyn_s_chamberlin

74. LEONARD HENRY LENZEN Born on 25 January 1890 in Volo, Lake County, Illinois. Leonard never married. He died in Volo on 5 February 1918. Burial at St. Peter's Cemetery in Volo. He died of a disease from Camp MacArthur, Waco, Texas while serving with the 127th Infantry Regiment, 32nd Infantry Division:
https://www.findagrave.com/memorial/35693619/leonard_henry_lenzen

75. MARIA CATHERINA "CATHERINE" B. LENZEN Born on 13 April 1892 in Volo, Lake County, Illinois. Catherine died in Waukegan, Lake County, Illinois on 28 February 1949. Burial at St. Mary Catholic Cemetery in Fremont Center, Lake County, Illinois:
https://www.findagrave.com/memorial/19508647/catherine-b_-behm

On 12 June 1913, CATHERINE LENZEN married MARCUS ADAM BEHM, son of ADAM BEHM (1851-1929) & MARIA HERTEL (1856-1945), at St. Mary Catholic Church in Fremont

Center, Lake County, Illinois. MARCUS ADAM BEHM was born on 18 April 1884 in Fremont Center. Marcus died in Fremont Center on 25 January 1971. Burial at St. Mary Catholic Cemetery in Fremont Center:
https://www.findagrave.com/memorial/19371991/marcus-a_-behm

CATHERINE & MARCUS were the parents of:
i. JAMES ISADOR BEHM (1914-1977)
ii. HELEN MARY BEHM HALL (1916-2004)
iii. RAYMOND J. BEHM (1918-1996)
iv. FRANCES ANN BEHM PADDOCK (1920-1985)
v. FLORENCE MARGARET BEHM MILLER (1922-1990)
vi. RALPH W. BEHM (1924-2012)
WW II Veteran, Purple Heart Recipient
https://www.findagrave.com/memorial/84258367/ralph_w_behm
vii. MARY ANN BEHM McREA-STEMWEDEL (1926-2002)
viii. ROSE BEHM SCHULZ-DOWE (1929-Living 27 January 2012)
ix. VIOLA V. BEHM PLOTZ (1931-2009) Twin of Virginia
x. VIRGINIA BEHM VASEY (1931-2016) Twin of Viola

76. JOSEPH FRANK LENZEN Born on 29 January 1895 in Volo, Lake County, Illinois. Joseph died on 7 May 1977 in Volo. Burial at St. Peter's Cemetery in Volo:
https://www.findagrave.com/memorial/48436837/joseph-f_-lenzen

On 21 June 1920, JOSEPH LENZEN married CLARA CECILIA ROSSDEUTCHER, daughter of Dr. KARL ROSSDEUTCHER (1864-1936) & LOUISE MARY DRACH (1867-1945), at St. Peter's Catholic Church in Volo, Lake County, Illinois. CLARA CECILIA ROSSDEUTCHER was born on 17 May 1899 in Volo, Lake County, Illinois. Clara died on 20 March 1938 in Waukegan,

Lake County, Illinois. Burial at St. Peter's Cemetery in Volo, Lake County, Illinois:
https://www. findagrave. com/memorial/35693524/clara-lenzen

JOSEPH & CLARA had no known children, per Census records.

13. JOHANN WILHELM (JOHN WILLIAM) MUELLER (MILLER) Born on 19 June 1857 in Richmond Township, McHenry County, Illinois. John Miller died in Spring Grove, McHenry County, Illinois on 1 July 1935. Burial at St. Peter's Cemetery in Spring Grove:
https://www. findagrave. com/memorial/117639887/john-w-miller

On 31 October 1878, JOHANN WILHELM MUELLER married MARGARETHA LENZEN, daughter of MICHAEL LENZEN (1825-1898) & ANNA MARIA ADOLPHI (1829-1909), at St. John the Baptist Catholic Church in Johnsburg, McHenry County, Illinois. MARGARETHA (MARGARET) LENZEN was born on 7 December 1852 in Heyroth, Dist. Vulkaneifel, Rhineland, Prussia. Margaret died in Spring Grove, McHenry County, Illinois on 28 December 1942. Burial at St. Peter's Cemetery in Spring Grove:
https://www. findagrave. com/memorial/117639888/margaret-miller

John and Margaret celebrated their Golden Anniversary in October 1928.

JOHN WILLIAM & MARGARET were the parents of:
- 77. i. MARIA (MARY) MILLER SEYMOUR (1880-1909)
- 78. ii. SUSANNA (ANNE MAE) MILLER (1882-1978)
- 79. iii. JOHN WILLIAM MILLER (1885-1960)
- 80. iv. WILLIAM J. MILLER (1887-1965)
- 81. v. KATHARINE MILLER McDANIEL (1890-1962)
- 82. vi. MICHAEL NICOLAS MILLER (1893-1974)
- 83. vii. BERNARD J. "BEN" MILLER (1897-1979)

77. MARIA (MARY) MILLER Born on 28 January 1880 in Spring Grove, McHenry County, Illinois. Mary died in Lake Geneva, Walworth County, Wisconsin on 18 February 1909, she was 29. Burial at St. Peter's Cemetery in Spring Grove, McHenry County, Illinois.

> *NOTE*: Excerpt from her obituary in Lake Geneva News, 25 February 1909: *"Mrs. Bert Seymour who was badly burned by flames from a gasoline stove several weeks ago died last Friday. . . . . She leaves behind a husband and two small children..."*
> https://www. findagrave. com/memorial/117639891/mary-seymour

On (about 1902), MARY MILLER married MILES NEWCOMB SEYMOUR, son of BURGE MILES SEYMOUR (1829-1899) & MARY ANN McCARTY (1834-1911). MILES NEWCOMB SEYMOUR was born in Lake Geneva, Walworth County, Wisconsin on 13 November 1877. Miles Newcomb Seymour died sometime after 18 April 1910.

MARY & MILES were the parents of:

i. **MARY SEYMOUR-MILLER SCHMITT (SMITH)** (1904-1977)

> *NOTE*: *Daughter of Mary MILLER and MILES NEWCOMB SEYMOUR, she may have been 'adopted' by her maternal grandparents, John Mueller (Miller) and Margaretha Lenzen, after the death of her mother Mary Miller Seymour. The grandparents changed her birth surname to Miller. She married John Bernard SCHMITT (SMITH).*
> https://www. findagrave. com/memorial/116796632/mary-smith

ii. **JOSEPH JOHN** (birth given name was WILLIAM HOWARD, surname SEYMOUR) **SEYMOUR-MILLER** (1908-1975), son of Mary MILLER and MILES NEWCOMB SEYMOUR.

NOTE: He may have been 'adopted' by his maternal grandparents, John Mueller (Miller) and Margaretha Lenzen, after the death of his mother Mary Miller Seymour. The grandparents changed his given name from William Howard to Joseph John, his surname from Seymour to Miller. He married Mildred Alberta SCHULTZ.
https://www.findagrave.com/memorial/76096031/joseph_j_seymour_miller

78. SUSANNE M. "ANNE MAE" MILLER Born on 22/23 November 1882 in Spring Grove, McHenry County, Illinois. Anne died in Woodstock, McHenry County, Illinois on 21 July 1978. Burial at St. Patrick Countryside Cemetery in McHenry, McHenry County, Illinois:
https://www.findagrave.com/memorial/172551066/anne-mae-miller

Excerpt from her obituary in **Woodstock Daily Sentinel, Monday, 24 July 1978, page 3:**

> "[ANNE MILLER] died at Woodstock Residence, age 95; Survivors include 2 grandchildren Douglas Miller of McHenry & Mrs. (Penny) Jack Zarnstorff of Twin Lakes, Wisconsin; two great-grandchildren and a brother, Ben Miller of McHenry. Preceded in death by a son Arthur, [no surname] on 9 January 1977; and brothers and sisters Kate McDaniels, *Mary Smith* (this is not a sister but a niece, the daughter of sister Mary Miller Seymour), *Mary Miller* (her sister Mary died in 1909), *Michael, John, William and Joseph Miller.*"

Child of ANNE MAE MILLER and NN:
i. **ARTHUR A. MILLER** Born on 30 April 1908 in Illinois. Arthur died in McCullom Lake, McHenry County, Illinois on 9 January 1977. Burial at St. Patrick Churchyard Cemetery in McHenry, McHenry County, Illinois:
https://www.findagrave.com/memorial/76570528/arthur_a_miller

ARTHUR A. MILLER married GLADYS L. NN. She was born in 1908. Gladys died on 22 March 1967 or October 1967, location unknown. Burial at St. Patrick Churchyard Cemetery in McHenry, McHenry County, Illinois:
https://www. findagrave. com/memorial/76570495/gladys_l_miller

ARTHUR & GLADYS NN were parents of:
i. DOUGLAS MILLER
ii. PENELOPE (PENNY) MILLER DOUGLAS-ZARNSTORFF

79. JOHANN WILLIAM (JOHN) MILLER Born on 5 May 1885 in McHenry County, Illinois. John died on 17 August 1960, location unknown. Burial at St. Peter's Cemetery in Spring Grove, McHenry County, Illinois
https://www. findagrave. com/memorial/117639889/john-w-miller

80. WILLIAM J. MILLER Born on 8 August 1887 in Spring Grove, McHenry County, Illinois. William never married. He died in Pistakee Bay, McHenry County, Illinois on 6 July 1965. Burial at St. Peter's Cemetery in Spring Grove, McHenry County, Illinois.

> *NOTE*: This was a local news item published in The McHenry Plaindealer newspaper: *"William Miller, his brothers Ben and Michael, were all arrested on 5 June 1919 in Spring Grove, McHenry County, Illinois, as draft dodgers."*
> https://www. findagrave. com/memorial/117639890/william-j-miller

81. KATHERINE MILLER Born on 26 June 1890 in McHenry County, Illinois. Katherine died in Waukegan, Lake County, Illinois on 29 November 1962. Burial at St. Patrick Churchyard Cemetery in McHenry, McHenry County, Illinois:
https://www. findagrave. com/memorial/76612582/katherine-mcdaniel

After 2 April 1930, KATHARINE MILLER married REUBEN BROUGHTON McDANIEL son of JACK NOLTON McDANIEL (1882-1916) & HENRIETTA HAND (1995-1967). Katharine was the 2nd wife of Reuben. REUBEN BROUGHTON McDANIEL was born on 27 June 1905 in Alabama. Reuben "Rubin" died in Chicago, Cook County, Illinois on 9 January 1963. Burial at Rosehill Cemetery in Chicago:
https://www. findagrave. com/memorial/187461910/rubin-mcdaniel

KATHERINE & REUBEN had no known children.

82. MICHAEL NICOLAS MILLER Born on 7 August 1893 in Johnsburg, McHenry County, Illinois. Michael died at his home in Spring Grove, McHenry County, Illinois on 12 December 1974.

> *NOTE: Michael's death was discovered by a neighbor on 12 December 1974. Burial at Cole Cemetery in Spring Grove:*
> https://www. findagrave. com/memorial/20155308/michael_n_miller

83. WILHELM BERNARD "BERNARD J. " MILLER Born on 20 March 1897 in Johnsburg, McHenry County, Illinois. BERNARD "BEN" MILLER died in McHenry, McHenry County, Illinois on 6 February 1979. Burial at Windridge Memorial Park in Cary, McHenry County, Illinois:
https://www. findagrave. com/memorial/119831042/bernard-j_-miller

On 25 December 1925, BERNARD J. "BEN" MILLER married SIGNA MARIE PACE nee ANDERSON, in Donaldson, Marshall County, Indiana. SIGNA MARIE ANDERSON was born in Sweden on 11 January 1897. Signa died in Illinois in May 1990. Burial at Windridge Memorial Park in Cary, McHenry County, Illinois:
https://www. findagrave. com/memorial/119831043/signa-m_-miller

NOTE: SIGNA ANDERSON married 1. LOUIS PACE on 18 January 1915 in Kane County, Illinois. She married 2. BEN MILLER on 25 December 1925. Her three children were not the biological children of Ben MILLER, they were children of Signa by her first marriage to LOUIS PACE.

Children:
i. ERNEST PACE-MILLER (b. abt 1916 - d. September 1942, WW II U. S. Navy casualty, received posthumous Purple Heart)
ii. FLORENCE PACE-MILLER PETERSON b abt 1918
iii. ESTHER PACE-MILLER KARBIN-RUDIN b abt 1921

14. MARIA "MARY" MUELLER Born on 17 August 1858 in Johnsburg, McHenry County, Illinois. Mary never married.. She died on 30 April 1896 in McHenry, McHenry County, Illinois. Burial at St. John the Baptist Cemetery in Johnsburg:
https://www. findagrave. com/memorial/71757700/mary-mueller

15. NIKOLAUS MUELLER Born on 28 October 1859 in Johnsburg, McHenry County, Illinois. Nikolaus never married. He died in Mitchell County, Iowa on 7 May 1883. Burial at St. John the Baptist Cemetery in Johnsburg, McHenry County, Illinois:
https://www. findagrave. com/memorial/76853468/nikolaus-mueller

16. PETER HENRY MUELLER (MILLER) Born on 22 July 1861 in Johnsburg, McHenry County, Illinois. Peter died in Stacyville, Mitchell County, Iowa on 17 December 1912. Burial at Stacyville Cemetery in Stacyville:
https://www. findagrave. com/memorial/74219384/peter-henry-miller

On 18 August 1891, PETER MUELLER (MILLER) married SUSANNA ALZINA PENNEY, daughter of WILLIAM R. PENNEY (1837-1919) & HANNAH MARTHA HALSEY (1841-1923), at Visitation Catholic Church in Stacyville, Mitchell County, Iowa. SUSAN ALZINA PENNEY was born on 18 August

1860 in Stacyville, Mitchell County, Iowa. Susan died in Stacyville on 11 January 1929. Burial at Stacyville Cemetery in Stacyville: https://www.findagrave.com/memorial/74219442/susan-alzina-miller

PETER & **SUSAN** were the parents of:
84. i. WILLIAM GEORGE MILLER (1893-1971)
     WW I Veteran, U. S. Army
85. ii. MARTHA BLANCHE MILLER BRENNECKE (1895-1982)
86. iii. BENJAMIN ROLFE MILLER (1897-1972)
87. iv. HARVEY JOHN MILLER (1899-1969)
88. v. JOSEPH HENRY MILLER (1900-1968)
89. vi. EMMA GRACE MILLER ADAMS (1902-1986)
90. vii. LUCILLE ALZINA MILLER FELPER (1905-1988)

84. WILLIAM GEORGE MILLER Born on 28 August 1893 in Stacyville, Mitchell County, Iowa. William died in Oconomowoc, Waukesha County, Wisconsin on 1 September 1971. Burial at Delafield Cemetery in Delafield, Waukesha County, Wisconsin. WW I Veteran.
https://www.findagrave.com/memorial/94984736/william-george-miller

Before the 1930 Census, WILLIAM GEORGE MILLER married FRIEDA STOCKS. FRIEDA STOCKS was born on 14 January 1899 in Wisconsin. Frieda died in Oconomowoc, Waukesha County, Wisconsin on 2 March 1970. Burial at Delafield Cemetery in Delafield, Waukesha County, Wisconsin:
https://www.findagrave.com/memorial/28395469/frieda_s_miller

WILLIAM and FRIEDA had no known children.

85. MARTHA BLANCHE MILLER Born on 12 January 1895 in Stacyville, Mitchell County, Iowa. Martha died in Friendship,

Adams County, Wisconsin on 19 June 1982. Burial at St. Henry Cemetery in Watertown, Dodge County, Wisconsin:
https://www.findagrave.com/memorial/7868897/martha_blanche_brennecke

In 1917, MARTHA BLANCHE MILLER married GEORGE FERDINAND BRENNECKE son of OTTO J. BRENNECKE (1865-1926) & BARBARA ANN RENZ (1871-1953). GEORGE FERDINAND BRENNECKE was born in Milwaukee, Milwaukee County, Wisconsin on 13 December 1890. George died in Friendship, Adams County, Wisconsin on 31 October 1972. Burial at St. Henry Cemetery in Watertown, Dodge County, Wisconsin:
https://www.findagrave.com/memorial/7867617/george_fernand_brennecke

Martha and George celebrated their Golden Anniversary in 1967.

MARTHA & GEORGE were parents of:
i. MILDRED SUSAN (MILLIE) BRENNECKE ERDMANN (1918-2001)
https://www.findagrave.com/memorial/144616743/mildred-s-erdmann
ii. KATHRYN GERTRUDE (KATE) BRENNECKE SCHROEDER (1920-2000)
https://www.findagrave.com/memorial/11619592/katherine_g_schroeder
iii. EVELYN IRENE (EVIE) BRENNECKE KACZOR (1922-2018)
https://www.findagrave.com/memorial/7908115/evelyn_irene_kaczor
iv. EUGENE WILLIAM BRENNECKE (1924-1980) WW II Veteran, Corporal U. S. Army:
https://www.findagrave.com/memorial/7912585/eugene_w_brennecke

v. GEORGE EDWARD BRENNECKE (1932-1994):
https://www.findagrave.com/memorial/144612504/george_edward_brennecke

vi. EDWARD (EDDIE) BRENNECKE (1933-Died before 19 October 2000)

86. BENJAMIN ROLFE MILLER Born on 4 April 1897 in Stacyville, Mitchell County, Iowa. Benjamin died in Watertown, Dodge County, Wisconsin on 25 May 1972. Burial at St. Henry Cemetery in Watertown, Dodge County, Wisconsin: https://www.findagrave.com/memorial/7912520/benjamin_r_miller

On 22 June 1920, BENJAMIN ROLFE MILLER married THERESA MARY FRANKE, daughter of BERNARD J. FRANKE (1868-1907) & CATHERINE RENZ (1866-1956), at St. Henry Catholic Church in Watertown, Dodge County, Wisconsin. THERESA MARY FRANKE was born in Sullivan, Jefferson County, Wisconsin on 24 December 1901. Therese died in Watertown, Dodge County, Wisconsin on 3 February 1992. Burial at St. Henry Cemetery in Watertown: https://www.findagrave.com/memorial/7912521/theresa_miller

BENJAMIN & THERESA were the parents of:

i. FLOYD HUBERT MILLER (1921-1986):
https://www.findagrave.com/memorial/7309404/floyd_hubert_miller

ii. MARION ELLEN MILLER CAYAN (1923-2009)

iii. EUNICE R. MILLER HENZE (1925-2010)

iv. KENNETH JOHN "BUD" MILLER (1928-1987)
WW II Veteran, U. S. Army

v. RITA CATHERINE MILLER MUIR (1931-2009)

vi. BENJAMIN CLIFFORD MILLER (1935-1989):
https://www.findagrave.com/memorial/42823931/benjamin_c_miller

87. HARVEY JOHN MILLER Born on 17 February 1899 in Stacyville, Mitchell County, Iowa. Harvey died in Randolph, Columbia County, Wisconsin on 27 October 1969. Burial at St. Henry Catholic Cemetery in Watertown, Dodge County, Wisconsin:
https://www.findagrave.com/memorial/8118684/harvey_john_miller

On 27 February 1919, HARVEY JOHN MILLER married 1. ELIZABETH ADAMS, daughter of JOHN ADAMS (1865-1937) & ANNA MARIA THOME (1865-1918), at Visitation Catholic Church in Stacyville, Mitchell County, Iowa. ELIZABETH ADAMS was born on 27 February 1901 in Stacyville. Elizabeth died in Randolph, Columbia County, Wisconsin on 23 June 1951. Burial at St. Henry Catholic Cemetery in Watertown:
https://www.findagrave.com/memorial/8118685/elizabeth_miller

HARVEY & ELIZABETH were the parents of the following known children:
i. JOSEPHINE MILLER FERNHOLZ (1921-2002)
ii. PETER WILLIAM MILLER (1922-2000)
iii. MARTIN LOUIS MILLER (1924-1941)
iv. AGNES IRENE MILLER (1927-1972)
v. MARGARET THERESA MILLER BEHM-ROWLANDS (1931-2002)
vi. RAYMOND MILLER (1944 - Living 31 January 2002)

HARVEY JOHN MILLER married 2. NORMA A. POLENSKY nee WEGNER (1908-1965), in September 1953.

88. JOSEPH HENRY MILLER Born on 19 August 1900 in Stacyville, Mitchell County, Iowa. Joseph died in Fort Atkinson, Jefferson County, Wisconsin on 25 September 1968. Burial at Hillside Cemetery, Whitewater, Walworth County, Wisconsin: https://www. findagrave. com/memorial/135240990/joseph-henry-miller

On 6 April 1925, Joseph Henry Miller married LOIS IVA ZIMMERMAN, daughter of OTTO HERMAN ZIMMERMAN (1883-1949) & CLARA RIDDLE (1885-1946), in Watertown, Dodge County, Wisconsin. LOIS ZIMMERMAN was born on 21 January 1907 in Sullivan, Jefferson County, Wisconsin. Lois died on 29 April 1979 in Fort Atkinson, Jefferson County, Wisconsin. Burial at Hillside Cemetery, Whitewater, Walworth County, Wisconsin:
https://www. findagrave. com/memorial/135241034/lois-i-miller

JOSEPH HENRY & LOIS were the parents of the following known children:

i. PAULINE JOYCE MILLER FERO (1926-2020)
ii. DARLENE MILLER DOBSON (1928-2010)
iii. JOSEPH MILLER (1931-2003)
iv. LAUREN RAYMOND MILLER (1936-2018):
https://nitardyfuneralhome. com/tribute/details/26230/Lauren-Miller/obituary. html
v. ALLEN RALPH MILLER (1939–2020):
https://www. findagrave. com/memorial/206508214/allen_ralph_miller
vi. JOAN E. MILLER GUNDERSON (1943-Living 23 January 2020)

89. EMMA GRACE MILLER Born on 4 September 1902 in Stacyville, Mitchell County, Iowa. Emma died in Osage, Mitchell

County, Iowa on 10 November 1986. Burial at Osage Cemetery in Osage:
https://www. findagrave. com/memorial/54175967/emma-grace-adams

On 1 May 1920, EMMA GRACE MILLER married ALBERT VERNIE "VERNIE" ADAMS, son of ALBERT ADAMS (1872-1942) & ROSE MAE ALBRIGHT (1873-1973), at Sacred Heart Catholic Church in Osage, Mitchell County, Iowa. ALBERT VERNIE ADAMS was born 15 February 1900 in Weaver City, Hamilton County, Iowa. Vernie died in Osage, Mitchell County, Iowa on 9 June 1976. Burial at Osage Cemetery in Osage:
https://www. findagrave. com/memorial/54175904/vernie-albert-adams

EMMA & ALBERT were the parents of:
i. ALZINA MAE ADAMS SHELDON (1921-2004)
ii. IRMA VIOLA ADAMS JEFFRIES (1924-2014):
https://www. findagrave. com/memorial/124772464/irma_v_jeffries
iii. FRIEDA ROSE ADAMS NABER (1932-2023):
https://www. legacy. com/us/obituaries/globegazette/name/frieda-naber-obituary?id=52432385

90. **LUCILLE ALZINA MILLER** Born on 26 May 1905 in Stacyville, Mitchell County, Iowa. Lucille died in Watertown, Dodge County, Wisconsin on 10 June 1988. Burial at Evangelical Lutheran Cemetery in Dodge County, Wisconsin:
https://www. findagrave. com/memorial/7721408/lucille-felper

On 27 June 1927, LUCILLE ALZINA MILLER married LELAND ANTHONY (LEE) FELPER, son of THOMAS KASPER FELPER (1868-1940) & NINA MAUDE RITTER (1876-1931), in Howard, Howard County, Iowa. LELAND ANTHONY "LEE" FELPER was

born in Osage, Mitchell County, Iowa on 21 June 1905. Lee died in Watertown, Dodge County, Wisconsin on 30 November 1972. Burial at Evangelical Lutheran Cemetery in Watertown, Dodge County, Wisconsin:
https://www.findagrave.com/memorial/7721507/lee-felper

LUCILLE & LEE were the parents of:
i. DOROTHY MAE FELPER LAMP
(Wallace G. 1915-1995)
(b 1922-Living 30 December 2009 in Utah)
ii. HARRY LLOYD FELPER (1927-1984)
iii. NORBERT LELAND FELPER
(1928-1988)
iv. SUSAN NINA FELPER ZOELLICK
(1929-2009):
https://www.findagrave.com/memorial/196071651/susan_nina_zoellick
v. INFANT SON (11 May 1932-11 May 1932)
vi. JEAN ANN FELPER ZILLMER
(1938-24 March 2009)
https://www.findagrave.com/memorial/274045737/jean_a_zillmer

17. ANNA MUELLER Born on 18 March 1863 in Johnsburg, McHenry County, Illinois. Anna died on 27 June 1870 in Johnsburg. Burial at St. John the Baptist Cemetery in Johnsburg:
https://www.findagrave.com/memorial/80284294/anna-mueller

18. SUSANNA MUELLER Born on 7 March 1865 in Johnsburg, McHenry County, Illinois. Susanna died on 30 September 1865 in

Johnsburg. Burial at St. John the Baptist Cemetery in Johnsburg: https://www.findagrave.com/memorial/80305104/susanna-mueller

19. ANNA MARIA "EMMA" MUELLER Born on 31 May 1867 in Johnsburg, McHenry County, Illinois. Emma died in McHenry, McHenry County, Illinois on 6 July 1932. Burial at St. Mary's Catholic Cemetery in McHenry:
https://www.findagrave.com/memorial/85222496/anna-maria-kennebeck

On 29 July 1903, EMMA MÜLLER married widower JOHN HENRY KENNEBECK, son of JOHANN BERNARD KERNEBECK (1807-1883) & ADELHEID HEMLING (1820-1891), at St. Mary's Catholic Church in McHenry, McHenry County, Illinois. JOHN HENRY KENNEBECK was born on 27 March 1862 in Pistakee, McHenry County, Illinois. John Henry died in McHenry on 7 January 1928. Burial at St. Mary's Catholic Cemetery in McHenry:
https://www.findagrave.com/memorial/71754215/john-henry-kennebeck

EMMA & JOHN HENRY were the parents of:
- 91. i. WILLIAM JOHN KENNEBECK (1904-1981)
- 92. ii. GENEVIEVE ELIZABETH KENNEBECK FOWLER (1906-1997)
- 93. iii. PAULINE JOSEPHINE KENNEBECK NIMSGERN (1908-1989)

91. WILLIAM JOHN KENNEBECK Born on 17 August 1904 in McHenry, McHenry County, Illinois. William died in McHenry

on 24 October 1981. Burial at St. Mary's Catholic Cemetery in McHenry:
https://www.findagrave.com/memorial/71754137/william-john-kennebeck

On 2 April 1929, WILLIAM KENNEBECK married MARY AGNES WILSON nee TURNER, daughter of BENJAMIN RUTHERFORD TURNER (1876-?) & JESSIE TORDOFF (1879-1966), in Elyria, Lorraine County, Ohio. MARY AGNES TURNER was born on 23 February 1901/02 in La Valle, Sauk County, Wisconsin. Mary died in Ravenna, Portage County, Ohio on 29 April 1942. Burial at Walnut City Cemetery in Baraboo, Sauk County, Wisconsin:
https://www.findagrave.com/memorial/157642673/mary-agnes-kennebeck

WILLIAM & MARY had no known children.

> *NOTE*: Mary had two children by her first marriage, a son ROBERT ARTHUR WILSON (1922-1937) and a daughter ELIZABETH JANE (BETTY) WILSON born 27 October 1920 in Bountiful, Utah. Her children in census records are recorded with the surname of Kennebeck, not Wilson.

92. **GENEVIEVE ELIZABETH KENNEBECK** Born on 3 January 1906 in McHenry, McHenry County, Illinois. Genevieve died in Oxnard, Ventura County, California on 13 June 1997. Burial at Holy Cross Cemetery in San Diego, San Diego County, California:
https://www.findagrave.com/memorial/85222252/genevieve-e_-fowler

On 20 June 1925, GENEVIEVE KENNEBECK married CHARLES ARTHUR FOWLER, son of CHARLES ARTHUR FOWLER & PARMELIA LOVELL. CHARLES ARTHUR FOWLER was born on 18 November 1901 in Denison, Grayson County, Texas. Charles died in La Mesa, San Diego County, California on 2 October 1985. Burial at Holy Cross Cemetery in San Diego, San Diego County, California:
https://www.findagrave.com/memorial/85222369/charles-arthur-fowler

GENEVIEVE & CHARLES had no known children.

93. PAULINE JOSEPHINE KENNEBECK Born on 17 April 1908 in McHenry, McHenry County, Illinois. Pauline died in McHenry on 14 November 1989. Burial at St. Mary's Catholic Cemetery in McHenry:
https://www.findagrave.com/memorial/69785519/pauline-j_-nimsgern

On 5 November 1931, PAULINE JOSEPHINE KENNEBECK married JOSEPH MATTHEW (JOE) NIMSGERN, son of FRANK NIMSGERN (1874-1922) & CATHERINE SCHAEFER (1877-1942), at St. Mary's Catholic Church in McHenry, McHenry County, Illinois. JOSEPH MATTHEW NIMSGERN was born on 9 July 1905 in Spring Grove, McHenry County, Illinois. Joseph died in McHenry, McHenry County, Illinois on 29 September 1983. Burial at St. Mary's Catholic Cemetery in McHenry:
https://www.findagrave.com/memorial/69785494/joseph-matthew-nimsgern

Joseph Nimsgern & Pauline Kennebeck
Louis Nimsgern (Best Man) &
Miss Martha May (Bridesmaid) both standing

PAULINE & JOSEPH were the parents of:
i. JOSEPH MATTHEW NIMSGERN
  (1932-2016) Never married
ii. JOAN MARY (JOANN) NIMSGERN LEON
  (1934-2012)
iii. WILLIAM BERNARD NIMSGERN Sr.
  (1936-2016) Korean War Veteran, U.S. Army
  Obituary, Northwest Herald, 24 March 2016
  https://www.findagrave.com/memorial/159956569/

20. MAGDALENA MUELLER Born on 29 January 1871 in Johnsburg, McHenry County, Illinois. Magdalena died on 11 March 1871 in Johnsburg. Burial at St. John the Baptist Cemetery

in Johnsburg:
https://www.findagrave.com/memorial/80304873/magdalena-mueller

21. ELIZABETH "LIZZIE" MUELLER Born on 6 February 1872 in Johnsburg, McHenry County, Illinois. Twin of Maria. Lizzie never married. She died at Northern Illinois Hospital in Elgin, Cook County, Illinois on 31 May 1919. The cause of death was pneumonia. Burial at St. John the Baptist Cemetery in Johnsburg, McHenry County, Illinois:
https://www.findagrave.com/memorial/76853512/lizzie-mueller

LIZZIE MUELLER

22. MARIA "MARY" MUELLER Born on 6 February 1872 in Johnsburg, McHenry County, Illinois. Twin of Elizabeth "Lizzie." Mary died on 20 August 1881 in Johnsburg. Burial at St. John the Baptist Cemetery in Johnsburg:
https://www.findagrave.com/memorial/76853495/mary-mueller

23. JOSEPHINA (JOSEPHINE) MUELLER Born on 3 June 1873 in Johnsburg, McHenry County, Illinois. Josephine died in Stacyville, Mitchell County, Iowa on 14 December 1956. Burial at Visitation Cemetery in Stacyville:
https://www.findagrave.com/memorial/37259238/josephine-mayer

On 17 November 1892, JOSEPHINE MUELLER married JOSEPH ROBERT MAYER, son of JOHANN MAYER (1828-1884) & MARIA ANNA SAUTHER (1826-1898), at Visitation Catholic Church in Stacyville, Mitchell County, Iowa. JOSEPH ROBERT MAYER was born on 8 August 1869 in Johnsburg, McHenry County, Illinois. Joseph died in Stacyville, Mitchell County, Iowa on 1 March 1953. Burial at Visitation Cemetery in Stacyville: https://www.findagrave.com/memorial/37259197/joseph-mayer

JOSEPHINE & JOSEPH were the parents of:
- 94. i. EDWARD WILLIAM MAYER (1893-1964) WW I Veteran, Army
- 95. ii. MICHAEL M. MAYER (1894-1955)
- 96. iii. ERNEST P. MAYER (1897-1968)
- 97. iv. RAYMOND NICHOLAS MAYER (1898-1973)
- 98. v. MARTHA MARY MAYER HEIMER (1901-1988)
- 99. vi. HERBERT L. MAYER (1904-1984)
- 100. vii. MARCELLA ANNA MAYER (1906-1971)
- 101. viii. LEONA MAYER (1910-2004)
- 102. ix. RALPH MAYER (1912-1972)

94. EDWARD WILLIAM MAYER Born on 28 August 1893 in Stacyville, Mitchell County, Iowa. Edward died in Santa Barbara, Santa Barbara County, California on 7 April 1964. Burial at Calvary Cemetery in Santa Barbara:
https://www.findagrave.com/memorial/169532947/edward-w_-mayer

On 6 February 1926, EDWARD WILLIAM MAYER married MAY AGNES PADDEN in Santa Barbara, California. MAY AGNES PADDEN was born on 16 December 1906 in Chicago, Cook County, Illinois. May died in Santa Barbara, Santa Barbara County, California on 23 May 1979. Burial at Calvary Cemetery in Santa Barbara:
https://www.findagrave.com/memorial/169533029/may-a_-mayer

EDWARD & MAY were the parents of one child, per 1940 census records:
i. JAMES EDWARD MAYER (1931-1984)

95. MICHAEL M. MAYER Born on 11 November 1894 in Stacyville, Mitchell County, Iowa. Michael Mayer never married. He died in Des Moines, Polk County, Iowa on 24 June 1955. Burial at Visitation Cemetery in Stacyville. Michael was a World War I Veteran, serving in France with the 47th CO 20th Army Engineers in 1918-1919. A military funeral was held at the Visitation Church in Stacyville. The American Legion and Auxiliary escorted the body. Pallbearers were World War I soldiers:
https://www.findagrave.com/memorial/37259302/michael-m-mayer

96. ERNEST PETER MAYER Born on 24 January 1897 in Stacyville, Mitchell County, Iowa. Ernest died in Stacyville on 7 February 1968. Burial at Visitation Cemetery in Stacyville:
https://www.findagrave.com/memorial/37264186/ernest-p-mayer

On 18 April 1923, ERNEST P. MAYER married MATHILDA LOECHER daughter of MATHIAS LOECHER (1866-1945) & MARY WEBER (1876-1942), at Visitation Catholic Church in Stacyville, Mitchell County, Iowa. MATHILDA LOECHER was born on 6 December 1900 in Stacyville, Mitchell County, Iowa. Mathilda died in Stacyville on 14 September 1992. Burial at Visitation Cemetery in Stacyville:
https://www.findagrave.com/memorial/37264086/mathilda-mayer

ERNEST & MATHILDA were the parents of:
i. EUGENE JOSEPH "GENE" MAYER (1924-2007)
   WW II Veteran, U. S. Army:
   https://www.findagrave.com/memorial/36968429/eugene_joseph_mayer

ii. **VERNON MATHIAS "VERNIE" MAYER (1927-2022):**
https://www.findagrave.com/memorial/239080468/vernon_mathias_mayer
iii. **ARLENE ISABELLA MAYER BROWN (EUGENE "GENE" 1932-1994) (1930-Living 19 April 2022)**
iv. **GLEN ALOIS MAYER (1934- 2022) Veteran, U. S. Army:**
https://www.findagrave.com/memorial/237921434/glen_alois_mayer

97. **RAYMOND NICHOLAS "ROY" MAYER** Born on 10 December 1898 in Stacyville, Mitchell County, Iowa. Raymond died in Stacyville on 8 March 1973. Burial at Visitation Cemetery in Stacyville:
https://www.findagrave.com/memorial/37259365/raymond-nicholas-mayer

On 19 February 1924, RAYMOND MAYER married CLARA HUEMANN/HEMANN (HEMANN became surname variation for some family members), daughter of NICHOLAS HUEMANN (1859-1943) & HELEN BLAKE (1867-1949), at Visitation Catholic Church in Stacyville, Mitchell County, Iowa. CLARA HUEMANN aka HEMANN was born on 15 December 1900 in Stacyville, Mitchell County, Iowa. Clara died in Stacyville on 7 April 1998. Burial at Visitation Cemetery in Stacyville:
https://www.findagrave.com/memorial/37259416/clara-mayer

RAYMOND & CLARA were the parents of:
i. **ROMANUS HERBERT "MAIN" MAYER (1925-2015) Korean War Veteran, U. S. Army:**
https://www.findagrave.com/memorial/149246596/romanus_herbert_mayer
ii. **ELMER JOSEPH MAYER (1927-2015) WW II Veteran, Corporal, U. S. Army:**
https://www.findagrave.com/memorial/151023026/elmer_joseph_mayer

    iii. CLARENCE MAYER (1930-1999)
        WW II Veteran, U. S. Army:
        https://www.findagrave.com/memorial/61606282/clarence_mayer
    iv. DARRELL FREDERICK MAYER (1932-2021):
    v. ALLAN ARTHUR "FUDDY" MAYER (1938-2023) Korean War Veteran, U. S. Army:
        Obituary: https://www.clasenjordan.com/obituary/allan-mayer

98. MARTHA MARY MAYER Born on 13 July 1901 in Stacyville, Mitchell County, Iowa. Martha died in Osage, Mitchell County, Iowa on 6 July 1988. Burial at Visitation Cemetery in Stacyville: https://www.findagrave.com/memorial/37259898/martha-mary-heimer

On 28 September 1921, MARTHA MAYER married ARTHUR JOHN HEIMER, son of JOSEPH H. HEIMER (1869-1956) & ELIZABETH SMITH (1876-1953), at Visitation Catholic Church in Stacyville, Mitchell County, Iowa. ARTHUR JOHN HEIMER was born on 31 October 1896 in Stacyville. Arthur died in Osage, Mitchell County, Iowa on 24 December 1961. Burial at Visitation Cemetery in Stacyville. WW I Veteran, U. S. Army, Private in 129th Base Hospital Unit:
https://www.findagrave.com/memorial/37259954/arthur-john-heimer

MARTHA & ARTHUR were parents of:
    i. IRENE JOSEPHINE HEIMER THOME (1922-1996)
    ii. WILMER JOSEPH "BUDDY" HEIMER (1924-1995)
        WW II Veteran, U. S. Army Air Corps:
        https://www.findagrave.com/memorial/38951196/wilmer_joseph_heimer
    iii. RALPH ARTHUR HEIMER (1927-1958)
    iv. LaVERNE PAUL HEIMER (1931-1983)
    v. LEON JEROME "CHARLIE" HEIMER (1936-2010):

www. legacy. com/us/obituaries/globegazette/
name/leon-heimer-obituary?id=22391004

99. HERBERT LEONARD MAYER Born on 10 January 1904 in Stacyville, Mitchell County, Iowa. Herbert died in Osage, Mitchell County, Iowa on 9 January 1984. Burial at Visitation Cemetery in Stacyville:
https://www. findagrave. com/memorial/37259573/herbert-l-mayerb

On 24 September 1929, HERBERT L. MAYER married AGNES CATHERINE GOERGEN, daughter of JOSEPH GOERGEN (1873-1951) & JOHANNA KOENIG (1877-1954), at St. John's Catholic Church in Johnsburg, Mower County, Minnesota. AGNES GOERGEN was born on 20 November 1908 in Johnsburg, Mower County, Minnesota. Agnes died in Osage, Mitchell County, Iowa on 1 April 1986. Burial at Visitation Cemetery in Stacyville:
https://www. findagrave. com/memorial/37259641/agnes-mayer

HERBERT & AGNES were the parents of:
i. MADONNA MARTHA "DONNA" MAYER MUESBY (1931-2016)
ii. SHIRLEY L. MAYER HACKENMILLER (1934-2007)
iii. JOHN H. "HERB" MAYER (1935-2017)
   Veteran, U. S. Army
iv. JANICE MARION MAYER HACKENMILLER (1938-2020)

100. MARCELLA MAYER Born on 5 August 1906 in Stacyville, Mitchell County, Iowa. Marcella never married. She died in Stacyville on 20 July 1971. Burial at Visitation Cemetery in Stacyville.
https://www. findagrave. com/memorial/37259699/marcella-mayer

101. LEONA MAYER Born on 9 December 1910 in Stacyville, Mitchell County, Iowa. Leona never married. She died in Osage, Mitchell County, Iowa on 3 December 2004. Burial at Visitation Cemetery in Stacyville.

> *"Leona grew up on the family farm east of Stacyville. Growing up, she was very active in 4-H, even having a grand champion holstein at the National Dairy Show in Memphis, Tennessee in 1927. Leona graduated from Visitation High School. After graduation, she worked in various homes in the Osage/Stacyville area. She worked as a telephone operator until Stacyville converted to dial telephones in the late 1950's. She then worked at the Stacyville Savings Bank until her retirement in 1975. Leona was a charter member of the Catholic Order of Foresters, serving in several offices, including treasurer for more than 40 years. She was very dedicated to her church. Leona was also a member of the American Legion Auxilliary for 45 years. After her retirement, she was able to enjoy gardening, especially roses and peonies. She was an avid sports fan, spending many summer nights watching 'Charlies Angels' at the softball diamond. She never missed the TV action of the Minnesota Twins, Chicago Bulls, Iowa Hawkeyes and, the last several years, Tiger Woods. Her other joys were spending time with the great- and great-great nieces and nephews, knitting and slot machines. She would never miss her Monday 'solo' game. She never complained and found good in everything. While she was never a mother, she was a special 'grandmother' to many and will be greatly missed."*
> https://www.findagrave.com/memorial/37259758/leona-mayer

102. RALPH MAYER Born on 9 November 1912 in Stacyville, Mitchell County, Iowa. Ralph died in Stacyville on 7 November 1972. World War II Veteran, PFC U. S. Army, 1289th Engineer Combat Battalion. Burial at Visitation Cemetery in Stacyville: https://www.findagrave.com/memorial/37259807/ralph-mayer

On 3 June 1941, RALPH MAYER married ANGELA MARIE MAUER, daughter of FRANK MAUER (1895-1975) &

ELIZABETH ADAMS (1898-1975), at Visitation Catholic Church in Stacyville, Mitchell County, Iowa. ANGELA MAUER was born on 10 April 1922 in Stacyville, Mitchell County, Iowa. Angela died in Stacyville on 24 August 2011. Burial at Visitation Cemetery in Stacyville.

> *NOTE*: Angela later remarried to RICHARD GINDER (1920-2010), on 17 September 1986.
> https://www. findagrave. com/memorial/ 75499294/angela-ginder

RALPH & ANGELA were the parents of:
i. THOMAS MAYER
ii. DEELYNN MAYER
iii. JOYCE MAYER WELCH
iv. ANTHONY (TONY) MAYER

Descendants of JACOB SCHMITT & ANNA GOEDERT through their daughter SUSANNA GOEDERT-SCHMITT (JOHANN MÜLLER):
16 Grandchildren (Bold Black)
48 Great-grandchildren (Fuchsia)
180 2x Great-grandchildren (Teal)

Chapter III

ANNA MARIA SCHMITT

3. ANNA MARIA SCHMITT Born on 2 October 1834 in Münk, Dist. Mayen, Rhineland, Prussia. Anna Maria was age 7 years at the time she and her parents Jacob and Anna, and her siblings Susanna age 9, Michael age 5 and Gertrud age 2 immigrated to America. Her mother Anna was with child on the ocean crossing to America, and she gave birth to a son Nicholas on 7 October 1841. Nicholas was the first child to be born in Johnsburg. The family departed from Port of Le Havre, France. They sailed for 38 days to reach New York, arriving at Port of New York on 2 August 1841 aboard the ship *Albany*. They traveled from New York to Chicago by train. From Chicago they journeyed by oxen-drawn wagon to what became the Village of Johnsburg. The Jacob Schmitt family traveled with the families of Nicolaus Adams (1799-1879) and Nicolaus Frett (1795-1844). They were the first three families, all from Dist. Mayen, Rhineland, Prussia, who founded the town of Johnsburg in McHenry County, Illinois.

ANNA MARIA died following childbirth on 26 January 1854 in Johnsburg, McHenry County, Illinois; she was 19. Burial at St. John the Baptist Cemetery in Johnsburg. Gravesite is unmarked: https://www.findagrave.com/memorial/41903976/anna-maria-freund

On 31 January 1853 ANNA MARIA SCHMITT married PETER FREUND, son of JOHANN PETER FREUND (1787-1861) & MARGARETHA HALFMANN (1800-1855), at St. John the Baptist Catholic Church in Johnsburg, McHenry County, Illinois. PETER FREUND was born 13 August 1825 in Lind, Dist. Mayen, Rhineland, Prussia. He died in Johnsburg, McHenry County, Illinois on 11 November 1900. Burial at St. John the Baptist Cemetery in Johnsburg:
https://www.findagrave.com/memorial/76942742/peter_freund

(Transcribed by MCIGS in 1985)
Early Records of St. John the Baptist Catholic Church
Johnsburg, McHenry County, Illinois
Volume I 1852-1868
Peter FREUND & Anna Maria SCHMITT
m 31 Jan 1853

> **NOTE**: *No witnesses were named in the transcription of the original church record, by MCIGS (McHenry County Genealogical Society) in 1985.*

ANNA MARIA & PETER were the parents of one child. Birth, Baptism and Death recorded at St. John the Baptist Catholic Church in Johnsburg.

24. SUSANNA FREUND Born on 26 January 1854 in Johnsburg, McHenry County, Illinois. Susanna died on 2 February 1854 in Johnsburg. Burial at St. John the Baptist Cemetery in Johnsburg.

> **NOTE**: *PETER FREUND later married 2. SUSANNA HESS (1836-1917), daughter of NICHOLAS HESS (1808-1882) & MARGARETHA KNOEPPELS (abt 1808-bef May 1847), on 13 February 1855 at St. John the Baptist Catholic Church in Johnsburg, McHenry County, Illinois. PETER FREUND & 2. SUSANNA HESS were the parents of 13 known children.*

Descendants of JACOB SCHMITT & ANNA GOEDERT through their daughter ANNA MARIA SCHMITT (PETER FREUND):
1 Grandchild (Bold Black)
0 Great-grandchildren (Fuchsia)
0 2x Great-grandchildren (Teal)

Chapter IV

GERTRUD SCHMITT

4. GERTRUD SCHMITT Born on 21 August 1839 in Münk, Dist. Mayen, Rhineland, Prussia. Gertrud was just 2 years of age at the time she and her parents Jacob and Anna, and her siblings, Susanna age 9, Anna Maria age 7 and Michael age 5, immigrated to America. Her mother Anna was with child on the ocean crossing to America, and she gave birth to a son Nicholas on 7 October 1841. Nicholas was the first child to be born in what became Johnsburg. The family departed from Port of Le Havre, France. They sailed for 38 days to reach New York, arriving at Port of New York on 2 August 1841 aboard the ship *Albany*. They traveled from New York to Chicago by train. From Chicago they journeyed by oxen-drawn wagon to what became the Village of Johnsburg. The Jacob Schmitt family traveled with the families of Nicolaus Adams (1799-1879) and Nicolaus Frett (1795-1844). They were the first three families, all from Dist. Mayen, Rhineland, Prussia, who founded the town of Johnsburg in McHenry County, Illinois.

GERTRUD died at the home of her daughter ANNA JUSTEN (JOSEPH H. JUSTEN) in McHenry, McHenry County, Illinois on 16 September 1902; she was 63. Burial on 19 September 1902 at St. Mary's Catholic Cemetery in McHenry:
https://www.findagrave.com/memorial/83377238/gertrude_schaefer
Obituary in **McHenry Plaindealer, 25 September 1902, Front page**:

"Gertrude Smith was born on Germany in October, 1839. At the age of three years her parents came to America and located at Johnsburgh where the subject of this sketch was raised to young womanhood. She was married later to Nicholas Schaefer who for some time worked for John W. Smith near Ringwood. About forty-two years ago Mr. Schaefer purchased the farm now occupied by Jos. H. Justen, where he and his wife resided up to about four years ago, when Mr. Schaefer was stricken with illness. He went to a hospital in Chicago for treatment and died while there. Mrs. Schaefer soon rented the farm and moved to McHenry where she continued to reside up to the time of her death. She had been under the doctor's care during the past eleven months, and a few weeks ago submitted to an operation which proved successful. The immediate cause of death was a severe cold on the lungs contracted while visiting at the old homestead last week.
Mrs. John Miller of this village is a sister of the deceased and a brother, Nicholas, lives in Minnesota. Three children are also living: Nicholas, of Oklahoma, Mrs. Henry Kennebeck and Mrs. Joseph Justen."

On 16 October 1856, when GERTRUD SCHMITT was 17, she married NIKOLAUS SCHAEFER, son of JOHANN SCHAEFER (1801-1867) & CATHARINA MARIA PULVERMACHER (1803-1883), at St. John the Baptist Catholic Church in Johnsburg, McHenry County, Illinois. NIKOLAUS SCHAEFER was born on 8 August 1831 in Münk, Dist. Mayen, Rhineland, Prussia. Nikolaus emigrated from Prussia (today Germany) with his parents and siblings. They arrived at the Port of New York on 11 January 1855 aboard the ship *Liverpool*. The Schaefer family traveled by train from New York to Chicago, then by ox-team to Johnsburg, McHenry County, Illinois; Nikolaus died at St. Alexander's Hospital in Chicago, Cook County, Illinois on 19 November 1897; he was 66. Burial on 21 November 1897 at St. Mary's Catholic Cemetery in McHenry, McHenry County, Illinois:

https://www.findagrave.com/memorial/84014441/nikolaus_schaefer
Obituary in McHenry Plaindealer, 24 November 1897, page 5.

(Transcribed by MCIGS in 1985)
Early Records of St. John the Baptist Catholic Church, Johnsburg, McHenry County, Illinois
Volume I: 1852-1868
Johann SCHAEFER & Gertrud SCHMITT
m 16 Oct 1856
Witnesses: Jacob SCHMITT & Johann HOEMANN

> NOTE: The Marriage License has their names recorded by the County Clerk as 'Nix SCHÄFFER' & 'Gertrud SMITH', the same document is also signed by the priest who performed the ceremony, Father Carolus. He recorded their names as 'Nix SCHÄFFER' & 'Gertrud SCHMITT.'

Nikolaus owned several farms in McHenry Township and in 1894 Nikolaus and Gertrude donated a portion of their farm land adjacent to Woodland Cemetery to be used for the St. Mary's Catholic Cemetery in McHenry:

(Transcribed by MCIGS 1997)
Northeastern Cemetery Index, McHenry Township: St. Mary's Cemetery.

> "This section of the county has been strongly Catholic since settlers first came here. [1836] As their numbers grew during the latter part of the 19th century, there was increased interest in starting a new church in McHenry for the German Catholics who had spread out from the Johnsburg area...in 1894 a new parish was set up by the Chicago Archbishop. The church operated out of an old school building until a regular house of worship could be built. In 1918 a fire completely destroyed this new church, and a new one was completed in 1919. In September of 1894 Nikolaus and Gertrud Schaefer donated an acre of their farm land adjacent to the Woodland Cemetery for the use of the McHenry German Catholic Society as a cemetery....in 1922 another one and a third acres were added and in

1966 Jacob and Rose Freund sold the church a portion of their farm land to be used for expansion to the west. They also provided the 70 foot square of land at the north edge of the cemetery where the columbarium was built...."

GERTRUD & NIKOLAUS were the parents of the following children. Their births and baptisms were recorded at St. John the Baptist Catholic Church in Johnsburg, McHenry County, Illinois. Their son Michael Schaefer's birth and baptism was recorded at St. Patrick Catholic Church in McHenry, McHenry County, Illinois.

25. i. **NICOLAUS PETER [GEORGE] "N. G." SCHAEFER [SCHAEFFER] (1857-1936)**
26. ii. **NICOLAUS "JOSEPH" SCHAEFER (1859-1899)**
27. iii. **ANNA SCHAEFER (1862-1863)**
28. iv. **JACOB SCHAEFER (1863-1864)**
29. v. **ANNA MARIA "EMMA" SCHAEFER KENNEBECK (1865-1899)**
30. vi. **JOHN A. SCHAEFER (1869-1900)**
31. vii. **ELISABETH SCHAEFER KENNEBECK (1871-1966)**
32. viii. **ANNA SCHAEFER JUSTEN (1874-1963)**
33. ix. **MATHIAS SCHAEFER (1877-1877)**
34. x. **MICHAEL SCHAEFER (1881-infant ?)**

Descendants of JACOB SCHMITT & ANNA GOEDERT
Grandchildren (Bold Black)
Great-grandchildren (Fuchsia)
2x Great-grandchildren (Teal)

25. **NICOLAUS PETER SCHAEFER** Born on 13 September 1857 in McHenry Township, McHenry County, Illinois. NICOLAUS PETER changed his name to GEORGE SCHAEFFER. Nicolaus

"George", "N. G." SCHAEFFER died in Omaha, Douglas County, Nebraska on 29 May 1936; he was 78. Burial at Holy Sepulchre Cemetery in Omaha:
https://www.findagrave.com/memorial/20170472/nicholas-g-schaeffer

Family lore passed down, has it that Nicolaus did not get along with his father, so he left home (never to return) by train (the local RR tracks run adjacent to the family farm off of McCullom Lake Road in McHenry) and settled in Omaha, Douglas County, Nebraska, eventually moving on to Oklahoma by 1895, and later, back to Omaha, Douglas County, Nebraska. He also thereafter, went by the given name of George, and added an 'f' to his surname making it Schaeffer. The name etched on his memorial stone is George Schaeffer.

On 5 October 1887 when NICOLAUS PETER "GEORGE" SCHAEFFER was 29, he married NELLIE HENNESSY of Omaha, Douglas County, Nebraska. NELLIE HENNESSY was born on 8 August 1861 in Canada. Nellie died in Omaha on 29 April 1933; she was 71. Burial at Holy Sepulchre Cemetery in Omaha:
https://www.findagrave.com/memorial/20170471/nellie-schaeffer

NICOLAUS "GEORGE", "N. G." & NELLIE were the parents of:

103. i. CATHERINE GERTRUDE SCHAEFFER WICKE (1889-1974)
104. ii. MILTON J. SCHAEFFER (1890-1918)
105. iii. ALICE ELIZABETH SCHAEFFER MATTHEWS (1891-1976)
106. iv. SUSANNA MARGARET SCHAEFFER SEWELL (1892-1978)
107. v. HENRY JOHN SCHAEFFER (1895-1897)
108. vi. MARY AGNES SCHAEFFER KIRBY (1897-1979)
109. vii. FREDERICK GEORGE SCHAEFFER (1900-1938)

103. CATHERINE GERTRUDE SCHAEFFER Born on 18 April 1889 in Omaha, Douglas County, Nebraska. Catherine died in Omaha, Douglas County, Nebraska on 5 May 1974; she was 84. Burial at Holy Sepulchre Cemetery in Omaha, Douglas County, Nebraska:
https://www.findagrave.com/memorial/140581844/catherine-gertrude-wicke

On 6 June 1917 when CATHERINE SCHAEFFER was 28, she married FREDERICK JOHN WICKE, son of ERNST WICKE (1858-1917) & LOUISE HINGST (1859-1897), in Omaha, Douglas County, Nebraska. FREDERICK JOHN "FRED" WICKE was born on 13 August 1886 in Emerson, Dixon County, Nebraska. Frederick "Fred" died in Omaha, Douglas County, Nebraska on 3 January 1966; he was 79. Burial at Holy Sepulchre Cemetery in Omaha:
https://www.findagrave.com/memorial/140581701/fred_john_wicke

CATHERINE & FRED were the parents of:
- i.   ALICE LOUELLEN WICKE McALLISTER (1918-2002)
- ii. CATHERINE GLADYS WICKE (1920-1992)
- iii. LEO WICKE (1921-1921)
- iv. BETTY ANN WICKE SIEPKER (1922-1993)
- v.   DAUGHTER WICKE (1923-1923)
- vi. JOAN MARIE WICKE SEVERIN (1926-2007) (twin of JOYCE)
- vii. JOYCE M. WICKE VOVK (1926-2015) (twin of JOAN)

104. MILTON J. SCHAEFFER Born on 29 October 1890 in Omaha, Douglas County, Nebraska. Milton died in Oklahoma City, Oklahoma on 10 October 1918; he was 28. Burial at Fairlawn Cemetery in Oklahoma City:
https://www.findagrave.com/memorial/50192303/milton_j_schaeffer

Obituary in the Oklahoma City Times, 11 October 1918, Front page.

On 27 January 1917, when MILTON J. SCHAEFFER was 27, he married CONSTANCE (CONNIE) ALBRIGHT (John Wesley) nee BUMGARNER, daughter of JOHN BRYAN BUMGARNER (1854-1918) & MARTHA SUSAN LAWS (1858-1941), in Logan County, Oklahoma. CONSTANCE BUMGARNER was born on 15 September 1889 in Kansas. Constance died in San Francisco, California on 14 August 1969; she was 79.

> *NOTE*: *Constance remarried to WILLIAM H. CHASE on 31 May 1921 in Oklahoma City, Oklahoma. Constance had only two known children, by her first marriage to John Wesley Albright, a son and daughter, who were said to have been adopted by her 3rd husband, William Chase.*

MILTON & CONSTANCE had no known children

105. **ALICE ELIZABETH SCHAEFFER** Born on 17 September 1891 in Omaha, Douglas County, Nebraska. Alice died in Omaha on 10 April 1976; she was 84. Burial at Calvary Cemetery in Omaha:
https://www.findagrave.com/memorial/191175534/alice_elizabeth_matthews+

On 23 June 1925 when ALICE ELIZABETH SCHAEFFER was 33, she married WILLIAM VALENTINE MATTHEWS son of STEPHEN ELWYN MATTHEWS (1859-1917) & ANNIE MAE BEACH (1859-1894), in Omaha, Douglas County, Nebraska. Alice was the 2nd wife of William. WILLIAM VALENTINE MATTHEWS was born 14 February 1891 in McDonald, Rawlins County, Kansas. William died in Omaha, Douglas County, Nebraska on 1 June 1957; he was 47. Burial at Calvary Cemetery in Omaha:

https://www.findagrave.com/memorial/191175451/william_valentine_matthews

ALICE & WILLIAM were the parents of:
i. WILLIAM STEPHEN MATTHEWS (1927-2009)
ii. MARY ALICE MATTHEWS (1930-2006)

> *NOTE*: Mary never married. Per her bio on her memorial at findagrave.com: *"From 1969 - 1993 she was on the staff at Southwest Minnesota State University in Marshall, Minnesota. Her position was Director of Publications and she retired with distinction."*

106. SUSANNA MARGARET "SUSIE" SCHAEFFER Born on 31 October 1892 in Omaha, Douglas County, Nebraska. Susan died in Omaha on 6 October 1978; she was 85. Burial at Holy Sepulchre Cemetery in Omaha:
https://www.findagrave.com/memorial/155506254/susan-margaret-sewell

On 14 June 1916 when SUSAN MARGARET SCHAEFFER was 23, she married HARRY LEROY JOHN SEWELL, son of GEORGE SEWELL (1868-1896) & MARY BONNEMIER (1871-1945), in Omaha, Douglas County, Nebraska. HARRY SEWELL was born on 8 February 1894 in South Bend, St. Joseph County, Indiana. Harry died in Omaha, Douglas County, Nebraska on 29 January 1965; he was 71. Burial at Holy Sepulchre Cemetery in Omaha:
https://www.findagrave.com/memorial/155506252/harry_leroy_john_sewell

SUSAN & HARRY were the parents of:
i. HARRY GEORGE SEWELL (1918-1970)
    WW II Army Signal Corps
ii. ELEANOR SEWELL KELLY (1920-2004)

iii. KATHLEEN SEWELL SCHARF (1923-2006)
iv. RITA SEWELL SCHAFFART (1926-1995)
v. JOSEPH M SEWELL (1932-1947)

107. HENRY JOHN SCHAEFFER Born on 10 August 1895 in Guthrie, Logan County, Oklahoma. Henry died in Guthrie on 10 January 1897.

108. MARY AGNES SCHAEFFER Born on 6 December 1897 in Guthrie, Logan County, Oklahoma. Mary died in Omaha, Douglas County, Nebraska on 29 September 1979; she was 81. Burial at Holy Sepulchre Cemetery in Omaha:
https://www.findagrave.com/memorial/98552051/mary-agnes-kirby

On 5 June 1929 when MARY AGNES SCHAEFFER was 32, she married WILLIAM MAURICE KIRBY son of MAURICE KIRBY (1854-1921) & ELLEN QUINN (1862-1944), in Omaha, Douglas County, Nebraska. WILLIAM MAURICE KIRBY was born on 31 October 1894 in Diller, Jefferson County, Nebraska. William died in Omaha on 26 July 1974; he was 79. Burial at Calvary Cemetery in Omaha, beside son Maurice William Kirby:
https://www.findagrave.com/memorial/132257594/william_maurice_kirby

MARY & WILLIAM were the parents of:
i. MAURICE WILLIAM (MORRIE) KIRBY (1931-1986)

109. FREDERICK GEORGE (FRED) SCHAEFFER Born on 21 January 1900 in Guthrie, Logan County, Oklahoma. Fred died in Omaha, Douglas County, Nebraska on 16 June 1938; he was 38. Burial at St. Mary Magdalene Cemetery in Omaha:
https://www.findagrave.com/memorial/83297342

In 1928 FRED SCHAEFER married LOUISE GUINOTTE, daughter of WALTER LEON GUINOTTE (b abt 1861-1935) & CATHERINE WALLER (1869-1941), in Nebraska. LOUISE GUINOTTE was born on 13 August 1904 in Omaha, Douglas County, Nebraska. Louise died in Lincoln, Lancaster County, Pennsylvania on 25 October 1980; she was 75. Burial at Hickman Cemetery in Hickman, Lancaster County, Nebraska.

> *NOTE*: Louise married 2. EDWARD J. KIRBY (1897-1978) on 18 April 1941.
> https://www.findagrave.com/memorial/81177536/louise_m_schaeffer_kirby

FRED & LOUISE were the parents of:
i. JACK F. SCHAEFFER (1929-1994)
   Korean & Vietnam War Veteran, ETC U.S. Navy
ii. JEANETTE SCHAEFFER MEYER (FRANCIS) (1931-2018)
    https://www.findagrave.com/memorial/189701069/jeanette_marie_meyer
iii. CATHERINE SCHAEFFER PIKE (EARL) (1930-2015)
    Obituary: https://www.bmlfh.com/obituary/catherine-pike
iv. BARBARA SCHAEFFER ELY (SAM) (1935-2011):
    https://www.findagrave.com/memorial/71398851/barbara-ann-ely

26. NICOLAUS "JOSEPH" SCHAEFER Born on 14 May 1859 in McHenry Township, McHenry County, Illinois. He died at his home in McHenry on 25 June 1899; he was 40. Burial at St. Mary's Catholic Cemetery, McHenry:
https://www.findagrave.com/memorial/71757757/joseph-n_-schaefer
Obituary on memorial page, and in McHenry Plaindealer, 30 June 1899, Front page.

On 25 November 1886 when JOSEPH SCHAEFER was 27, he married ELIZABETH SABEL daughter of CHRISTIAN SABEL (1841-1908) & ANNA MARIA SCHMITT (1848-1941), at St. John the Baptist Catholic Church in Johnsburg, McHenry County, Illinois. ELIZABETH SABEL was born on 25 July 1868 in Volo, Lake County, Illinois. ELIZABETH SABEL SCHAEFER remarried to THEODORE WINKELS (1877-1964). She died in McHenry, McHenry County, Illinois on 13 December 1940; she was 72. Burial at St. Mary's Catholic Cemetery in McHenry: https://www.findagrave.com/memorial/61590680/elizabeth-k-winkel

JOSEPH & ELIZABETH were the parents of:
110. i. GERTRUDE SCHAEFER WORMLEY (1887-1962)
111. ii. MAGDALENA "LILLIAN" (LENA) SCHAEFER PETERSEN (1890-1983)
112. iii. HENRY J. "BUB" SCHAEFER (1892-1980)
113. iv. MARY "MAYME" SCHAEFER PERKINSON (1896-1979)

110. GERTRUDE SCHAEFER Born on 3 October 1887 in McHenry Township, McHenry County, Illinois. Gertrude died in McHenry, McHenry County, Illinois on 10 December 1962; she was 74. Burial at St. Mary's Catholic Cemetery in McHenry, McHenry County, Illinois:
https://www.findagrave.com/memorial/69785134/gertrude-wormley
Obituary on memorial, and in McHenry Plaindealer, 13 December 1962, page 8.

On 9 February 1914 when GERTRUDE SCHAEFER was 27, she married widower JESSE WORMLEY, son of JOHN B. WORMLEY & MARY GRAHAM (1853-1932), in Illinois. JESSE WORMLEY was born 30 April 1875 in Mendota, LaSalle County, Illinois. Jesse died in McHenry, McHenry County, Illinois on 28 January 1953; he was 77. Burial at St. Mary's Catholic Cemetery in McHenry:
https://www.findagrave.com/memorial/69785117/jesse-wormley
Obituary on memorial and in McHenry Plaindealer, 5 February 1953, Front page.

GERTRUDE & JESSE were the parents of:
i. DOROTHY WORMLEY LEE (1912-1978)

III. MAGDALENA "LILLIAN" SCHAEFER Born on 8 February 1890 in McHenry Township, McHenry County, Illinois. Lillian died in Chicago, Cook County, Illinois on 16 January 1983; she was 92. Burial at St. Mary's Catholic Cemetery in McHenry, McHenry County, Illinois:
https://www.findagrave.com/memorial/69785151/lillian-petersen

On 25 January 1913 when LILLIAN SCHAEFER was 22, she married JOHN CHRISTIAN PETERSEN, son of CHRISTIAN PETERSEN (1854-1937) & PETRIE JOHNSON, at St. Mary's Catholic Church in McHenry, McHenry County, Illinois. JOHN CHRISTIAN PETERSEN was born in Chicago, Cook County, Illinois on 14 March 1880. John died in Chicago on 5 January 1943; he was 62. Burial at Mt. Olive Cemetery, Chicago, Cook County, Illinois:
https://www.findagrave.com/memorial/188233963/john-christian-petersen

LILLIAN & JOHN were the parents of no known children per the Census records.

112. HENRY JOSEPH "BUB" SCHAEFER Born on 10 September 1892 in McHenry Township, McHenry County, Illinois. Henry died in McHenry on 8 January 1980; he was 87. Burial at St. Mary's Catholic Cemetery in McHenry:
https://www.findagrave.com/memorial/70040743/henry-j-schaefer

On 3 August 1918 when HENRY "BUB" SCHAEFER was 25 he married GERTRUDE BROUGHTON, daughter of GEORGE McCLELLAN BROUGHTON (1866-1950) & CATHERINE BLACKBURN (1869-1938), in Winnebago, Winnebago County,

Illinois. GERTRUDE BROUGHTON was born on 10 August 1899 in Wauconda, Lake County, Illinois. Gertrude died in Illinois on 3 June 1966; she was 67. Burial at St. Mary's Catholic Cemetery in McHenry, McHenry County, Illinois:
https://www.findagrave.com/memorial/70040752/gertrude-e-schaefer

HENRY & GERTRUDE were the parents of:
i. EARL GORDON SCHAEFER (1920-1993)
ii. ROBERT L. SCHAEFER (1925-1969)
iii. DONALD HENRY SCHAEFER (1926-2018)
   WW II Veteran, U.S. Army, Aerial Photographer

"Donald H. Schaefer, 91, of Arlington Heights and formerly of Springfield, peacefully passed away on February 25, 2018, living a full and complete life of love and family. He was born December 8, 1926 in McHenry, Illinois, the third son of Henry B. and Gertrude Broughton Schaefer. He was educated at McHenry schools, playing football and the French horn, and as a teen worked at the ice cream shop at the McHenry Dairy and attained the rank of Eagle Scout. His 15th birthday coincided with the bombing at Pearl Harbor, but it was another two years before he joined the Army and was trained as an aerial photographer. After the war, he went to work for Illinois Bell. He started as a lineman in Woodstock and worked as an operations engineer in McHenry, Joliet, Springfield and Chicago during a career that spanned nearly 40 years. He also served as an Alderman for the City of McHenry. Don and Sis resided in Springfield from 1966 until 1985. During those years he was active in Christ the King Parish and participated in many golf and bowling leagues. He was also a member of the first Springfield Railroad Relocation Authority. He retired in 1985, but remained busy with marketing and volunteer positions. He was an active member of Telephone Pioneers of America. All through his life was his constant companion and soulmate of 65 years, Estelle 'Sis' Schaefer. A Chicago girl who summered on the Chain-of-Lakes in McHenry, they met and married five years later on January 24, 1953. God blessed them with five children, Mary (Dennis) Mahoney, Donald Jr. (Mary), James (Marilyn), Thomas (Jana), and Phillip (Kate); 11 grandchildren, Molly (William) Opal, Peter Mahoney, Michael Mahoney, Ali

Mahoney, Geoffrey (Kinga) Schaefer, Melissa Schaefer, Maggie (Keenan) Gilpin, Mickey Schaefer, Nicholas Schaefer, Megan Schaefer and Amy Schaefer; and a great-granddaughter, Mary Grace Opal. He was preceded in death by his parents and two brothers, Earl and Robert Schaefer."
https://www.findagrave.com/memorial/187629740/donald-henry-schaefer

113. MARY "MAYME" SCHAEFER Born in July 1896 in McHenry, McHenry County, Illinois. Mary died in Evanston, Cook County, Illinois on 5 October 1979; she was 83. Burial at All Saints Cemetery in Des Plaines, Cook County, Illinois:
https://www.findagrave.com/memorial/188329346/mary-perkinson

On 1 March 1919 when MARY SCHAEFER was 23, she married WILLIAM JAMES PERKINSON, son of JAMES H. PERKINSON (1860-1949) & ANNA C. STRANG (1863-1910), in Chicago, Cook County, Illinois. WILLIAM JAMES PERKINSON was born on 15 May 1891 in Chicago, Cook County, Illinois. William died in Chicago on 4 April 1971; he was 79. Burial at All Saints Cemetery in Des Plaines, Cook County, Illinois:
https://www.findagrave.com/memorial/188329246/william-james-perkinson

MARY & WILLIAM were the parents of:
i. MARILYN PERKINSON (1930-

27. ANNA SCHAEFER Born on 6 June 1862 in McHenry Township, McHenry County, Illinois, died on 19 March 1863 in McHenry Township. Burial at St. John the Baptist Cemetery in Johnsburg, McHenry County, Illinois:
https://www.findagrave.com/memorial/80307298/anna-schaefer

28. JACOB SCHAEFER Born on 3 September 1863 in McHenry Township, McHenry County, Illinois, died on 2 September 1864

in McHenry Township. Burial at St. John the Baptist Cemetery in Johnsburg, McHenry County, Illinois:
https://www.findagrave.com/memorial/80307470/jacob-schaefer

29. ANNA MARIA "EMMA" SCHAEFER Born on 2 August 1865 in McHenry Township, McHenry County, Illinois. Emma died following childbirth on 6 June 1899 in Ringwood, McHenry County, Illinois; she was 33. Burial at St. Mary's Catholic Cemetery in McHenry, McHenry County, Illinois:
https://www.findagrave.com/memorial/71754180/anna-maria-kennebeck
Obituary on memorial, and in McHenry Plaindealer, 9 June 1899, Front page.

On 5 November 1885 when EMMA SCHAEFER was 20, she married JOHN HENRY KENNEBECK, son of JOHANN BERNARD KERNEBECK (1807-1883) & ADELHEID HEMLING (1820-1891), at St. John the Baptist Catholic Church in Johnsburg, McHenry County, Illinois. JOHN HENRY KENNEBECK was born on 27 March 1862 in Pistakee, McHenry County, Illinois. John Henry died in McHenry, McHenry County, Illinois on 7 June 1928; he was 66. Burial at St. Mary's Catholic Cemetery in McHenry:
https://www.findagrave.com/memorial/71754215/john-henry-kennebeck
Obituary on memorial, and in McHenry Plaindealer, 12 January 1926, Front page.

JOHN HENRY KENNEBECK later married the cousin of his first wife, 2. EMMA MUELLER, daughter of JOHANN MUELLER (1821-1908) & SUSANNA SCHMITT (1832-1910), on 29 July 1903 at St. Mary's Catholic Church in McHenry, McHenry County, Illinois.

They were the parents of three children:
WILLIAM JOHN KENNEBECK (MARY AGNES TURNER)
GENEVIVE ELIZABETH KENNEBECK (CHARLES ARTHUR FOWLER)
PAULINE JOSEPHINE KENNEBECK (JOSEPH MATTHEW NIMSGERN)

> *NOTE*: *See Chapter II, Susanna Schmitt.*

EMMA SCHAEFER & JOHN HENRY were the parents of:
114. i. **NICHOLAS KENNEBECK** (1886-1947)
115. ii. **HEINRICH KENNEBECK** (1887-Infant)
116. iii. **ANNA MARIA KENNEBECK BOLEY** (1889-1958)
117. iv. **ELISABETH KENNEBECK ANDERSON** (1890-1965)
118. v. **KATHERINE ANNA KENNEBECK WIENKE** (1891-1952)
119. vi. **HEINRICH JOSEPH KENNEBECK** (1893-1960)
120. vii. **BERNARD JOSEPH KENNEBECK** (1895-1960)
121. viii. **CECEILIA KENNEBECK** (1899-1899)

114. NICHOLAS KENNEBECK Born 15 August 1886 in Ringwood, McHenry County, Illinois. Nicholas died in Woodstock, McHenry County, Illinois on 4 July 1947; he was 61. Burial at St. Mary's Catholic Cemetery in McHenry, McHenry County, Illinois.

> *NOTE*: *Nicolaus died from injuries he suffered in a fall from a barn hayloft on the farm of his father-in-law (GEORGE SCHEID) in Griswold Lake, McHenry County, Illinois. He died at the Woodstock Hospital in Woodstock:*
> https://www.findagrave.com/memorial/66844653/nicholas-kennebeck
> *Obituary on memorial and in McHenry Plaindealer.*

On 12 October 1910 when NICHOLAS KENNEBECK was 24, he married LAURA KATHRYN SCHEID, daughter of GEORGE SCHEID (1864-1956) & MARIE CATHERINE KLASSEN

(GLOSSON) (1865-1940), at St. Mary Catholic Church in McHenry, McHenry County, Illinois. LAURA KATHRYN SCHEID was born on 10 December 1891 in Chicago, Cook County, Illinois. Laura died in Orlando, Orange County, Florida on 27 March 1955; she was 64. Burial at St. Mary's Catholic Cemetery in McHenry, McHenry County, Illinois: https://www.findagrave.com/memorial/66844538/laura-kathryn-kennebeck

LAURA SCHEID & NICOLAUS KENNEBECK

NICHOLAS & LAURA were parents of:
  i.   CLARA CATHRYN KENNEBECK NESTER (1911-1997)
  ii. ELMER GEORGE KENNEBECK (1914-1980)
  iii. HAROLD J. KENNEBECK (1917-1919)

115. **HEINRICH KENNEBECK** Born on 19 October 1897 in Ringwood, McHenry County, Illinois. Heinrich died as an infant, date not known:
https://www.findagrave.com/memorial/149502239/heinrich-kennebeck

116. **ANNA MARIA KENNEBECK** Born on 17 January 1889 in Ringwood, McHenry County, Illinois. Anna died in McHenry, McHenry County, Illinois on 20 April 1958; she was 69. Burial at St. Mary's Catholic Cemetery in McHenry:
https://www.findagrave.com/memorial/68731443/anna-maria-boley
Obituary on memorial, and in McHenry Plaindealer, 24 April 1958, page 8.

On 22 January 1908, when ANNA MARIA KENNEBECK was 20, she married CHRISTOPHER GOTTLIEB "PAT" BOLEY, son of GOTTLIEB FREDERICH BOLEY (1844-1900) & JOSEPHINA ANNA PYTLIKOVA (1847-1936), at St. Mary's Catholic Church in McHenry, McHenry County, Illinois. PAT BOLEY was born on 16 March 1883 in McHenry, McHenry County, Illinois. Pat died in Ringwood, McHenry County, Illinois following a tragic auto accident on 23 December 1959; he was 76. Burial at St. Mary's Catholic Cemetery in McHenry:
https://www.findagrave.com/memorial/68731408/gottlieb-c-boley
Obituary in McHenry Plaindealer, 30 December 1959, Front page.

Anna and Pat celebrated their Golden Anniversary in January 1958.

ANNA & PAT were the parents of:
i. CHARLES JOHN BOLEY (1909-1910)
ii. KENNETH NICHOLAS BOLEY (1914-1999)

117. **ELIZABETH PAULINE KENNEBECK** Born 21 May 1890 in Ringwood, McHenry County, Illinois. Elizabeth died in Chicago, Cook County, Illinois on 7 January 1965; she was 74. Burial at St.

Joseph's Cemetery in River Grove, Cook County, Illinois: https://www.findagrave.com/memorial/85213907/elizabeth-anderson

On 26 September 1910 when ELIZABETH KENNEBECK was 20, she married ALBERT FRANKLIN ANDERSON, son of FREDERICH ANDERSON (1841- aft 20 April 1910) & CHRISTINA MARGARET PETERSON (1849-1929), at St. Mary's Catholic Church in Woodstock, McHenry County, Illinois. ALBERT FRANKLIN ANDERSON was born on 14 February 1885 in Belleville, Monroe Township, Green County, Wisconsin. Albert died in Norwood Park, Cook County, Illinois on 22 March 1959; he was 74. Burial at St. Joseph's Cemetery in River Grove, Cook County, Illinois:
https://www.findagrave.com/memorial/85214820/albert-f_-anderson

> *NOTE*: "Elisabeth's father John Henry Kennebeck, did not approve of her marriage to "a Non-German, Non-Catholic, Non-Local Man". Source: Per the bio of Elisabeth's half-sister, Genevieve Kennebeck Fowler.

ELISABETH & ALBERT were the parents of:
i. FREDERICH JOHN ANDERSON (1911-1976)
ii. EUGENE ALBERT ANDERSON (1912-1990)
iii. ZARA KATHRYN ANDERSON DE MICHAELS (1915-2008)
iv. CALVIN RAYMOND ANDERSON (1924-1967)
v. ELISABETH JANE ANDERSON STAKE (1930-)

118. KATHERINE (KATHRYN) KENNEBECK Born on 14 July/ August 1891 in Ringwood, McHenry County, Illinois. Kathryn died in Chicago, Cook County, Illinois on 14 May 1952; she was 61. Burial at St. Joseph's Cemetery in River Grove, Cook County, Illinois:
https://www.findagrave.com/memorial/85221425/kathryn-a_-wienke
Obituary on memorial and in McHenry Plaindealer, 15 May 1952, Front page.

On 25 November 1917, when KATHERINE KENNEBECK was 25, she married RAYMOND MARTIN WIENKE, son of WILLIAM J. WIENKE (1863-1919) & ELIZABETH SOPHIA SHUETT (1862-1945), at St. Mary's Catholic Church in Woodstock, McHenry County, Illinois. RAYMOND WIENKE was born on 4 August 1892 in Caledonia, Boone County, Illinois. Raymond died in Coral Gables, Dade County, Florida on 17 November 1947; he was 55. Burial at St. Joseph's Cemetery in River Grove, Cook County, Illinois:
https://www.findagrave.com/memorial/85221619/raymond-martin-wienke

KATHRYN & RAYMOND were the parents of:
i.   HENRY RAYMOND WIENKE (1918-2000)
ii. WILLIAM JOHN WIENKE (1924-2004)
     WW II Veteran, Army Air Corps
iii. MARY ELIZABETH WIENKE YOUNGS (1932-)

119. HEINRICH JOSEPH KENNEBECK Born on 26 September 1893 in Ringwood, McHenry County, Illinois. Henry died in Elgin, Kane County, Illinois on 10 March 1960; he was 66. Burial at St. Mary's Catholic Cemetery in McHenry, McHenry County, Illinois:
https://www.findagrave.com/memorial/69877275/henry-j-kennebeck
Obituary on memorial, and in McHenry Plaindealer, 17 March 1960, page 5.

> *NOTE*: *This Henry Joseph Kennebeck is sometimes confused with his cousin ("Hank"), also named Henry Joseph, who was born in July 1896, son of Henry Kennebeck, who was the brother of John Henry Kennebeck.*

On 20 October 1920 when HENRY JOSEPH KENNEBECK was 26, he married HELENA MARIA FREUND, daughter of

MICHAEL FREUND (1860-1925) & SUSANNA HILLER (1861-1923), at St. Mary's Catholic Church in McHenry, McHenry County, Illinois. HELENA FREUND was born on 2 December 1896 in Johnsburg, McHenry County, Illinois. Helena died in Libertyville, Lake County, Illinois on 28 July 1966; she was 70. Burial at St. Mary's Catholic Cemetery in McHenry: https://www.findagrave.com/memorial/69877292/helena-maria-kennebeck

Helena Freund & Henry Kennebeck

HENRY & HELENA were the parents of:

i. GERALDINE ANNE KENNEBECK LLOYD-WAGNER (1921-1998)
  ii. DORIS JEAN KENNEBECK ZERBY (1922-1998)
  iii. DONALD RAYMOND "SMOKEY" KENNEBECK (1927-1995) WW II Veteran, Tech 5 U.S. Army
  iv. JAMES ALLEN KENNEBECK (1932-2006) Korean War Veteran, Corp. U.S. Army
  v. RICHARD KENNEBECK (1936-1936)

120. BERNARD JOSEPH "BEN" KENNEBECK Born on 30 November 1895 in Ringwood, McHenry County, Illinois. Ben died in McHenry, McHenry County, Illinois on 28 October 1960; he was 64. Burial at St. John the Baptist Cemetery in Johnsburg, McHenry County, Illinois:
https://www.findagrave.com/memorial/77030141/ben_joseph_kennebeck
Obituary on memorial, and in McHenry Plaindealer, 3 November 1960, page 15.

On 3 October 1917, when BEN KENNEBECK was 21, he married DOROTHEA "DORA" SCHUMACHER, daughter of JACOB B. SCHUMACHER (1866-1947) & SUSANNA ROSA FREUND (1867-1950), at St. John the Baptist Catholic Church in Johnsburg. DORA SCHUMACHER was born on 19 May 1899 in Johnsburg, McHenry County, Illinois. Dora died in McHenry on 20 November 1977; she was 78. Burial at St. John the Baptist Cemetery in Johnsburg:
https://www.findagrave.com/memorial/77030166/dorothy_b_kennebeck

BEN & DORA were the parents of:
  i. EDNA ROSE KENNEBECK (1918-1934)
  ii. DONALD J. KENNEBECK (1920-1921)
  iii. DANIEL JACOB KENNEBECK (1920-2005)

iv. LORRAINE D. KENNEBECK HOLM (1922-2005)
v. JEANETTE KENNEBECK GAYLORD (1923-1999)
vi. RAYMOND HENRY KENNEBECK (1924-1961)
vii. BERNARD NICHOLAS KENNEBECK (1926-2011) Korean War Veteran, U.S. Army
viii. ARTHUR FLOYD "BUD" KENNEBECK (1927-2009)

121. CECELIA KENNEBECK Born and died at birth on 6 June 1899 in Ringwood, McHenry County, Illinois. Buried with her mother **Emma SCHAEFER KENNEBECK** who died following the birth of Cecelia.

30. JOHN A. SCHAEFER Born on 22 January 1868/1869 in McHenry Township, McHenry County, Illinois. He died at his home in McHenry, McHenry County, Illinois on 24 March 1900 following spinal injuries suffered in a fall from his wagon while returning from Wauconda Mills, Wauconda, Lake County, Illinois; he was 31. Burial at St. Mary's Catholic Cemetery in McHenry:
https://www.findagrave.com/memorial/61571371/john_a_schaefer
Obituary on memorial, and in McHenry Plaindealer, 29 March 1900, Front page.

On 30 January 1895 when JOHN SCHAEFER was 21, he married CATHARINA MAGDALENA "MAGDALENA" BUCH, daughter of JOSEPH BUCH (1838-1898) & CATHARINA SCHNORR (1830-1904), at St. John the Baptist Catholic Church in Johnsburg, McHenry County, Illinois. MAGDALENA BUCH was born on 30 May 1871 in McHenry, McHenry County, Illinois. MAGDALENA died in McHenry on 17 August 1948; she was 77. Burial at St. Mary's Catholic Cemetery in McHenry.

On 6 November 1902, MAGDALENA remarried to NICHOLAS BOHR (1862-1963), son of MICHAEL BOHR (1833-1880) & ANNA CATHARINA SCHMITT (1841-1880), at St. Mary's

Catholic Church in McHenry. They were the parents of three children; GEORGE BOHR (1905-1966), GENEVIVE JULIA BOHR SENGSTOCK (1907-1995) & ERNEST MICHAEL BOHR (1916-2003):
https://www.findagrave.com/memorial/15894733/magdalena_k_bohr
Obituary on memorial, and in McHenry Plaindealer, 19 August 1948, Front page.

JOHN & MAGDALENA were the parents of:
122. i. CATHARINA "KATIE" PAULINE SCHAEFER (1897-1907)
123. ii. JOHN WILLIAM "WILLIAM" SCHAEFER (1899-1955)

122. **CATHARINA "KATIE" PAULINE SCHAEFER** Born on 11 March 1897 in McHenry, McHenry County, Illinois. Katie died on 24 June 1907 in McHenry, McHenry County, Illinois. Young Katie was a victim of measles. Burial Saint Mary's Catholic Cemetery in McHenry, McHenry County, Illinois.
https://www.findagrave.com/memorial/61572242/katie_schaefer
Obituary on memorial page, and in McHenry Plaindealer, 27 June 1907, Front page.

123. **JOHN WILLIAM "WILLIAM" SCHAEFER** Born on 6 December 1899 in McHenry, McHenry County, Illinois. William died in Melbourne, Brevard County, Florida on 20 February 1955; he was 55. Burial at St. Mary's Catholic Cemetery in McHenry.

> **NOTE**: *William Schaefer was just 3 months old when his father John Schaefer died. William was a WW I Veteran, PFC 23rd RCT CO GEN SVC Infantry.*
> https://www.findagrave.com/memorial/61331710/william_schaefer

Obituary on memorial, and in McHenry Plaindealer, 24 February 1955, page 5.

On 22 September 1920, WILLIAM SCHAEFER married CATHERINE "KATIE" MIDDENDORF, daughter of HENRY MIDDENDORF (1867-1934) & ELISABETH SCHMIDT (1876-1928), in St. Louis, St. Louis County, Missouri. CATHERINE MIDDENDORF was born on 2 April 1903 in Missouri. Katie died in Antioch, Lake County, Illinois on 28 February 1987; she was 83. Burial at St. Mary's Catholic Cemetery in McHenry, McHenry County, Illinois:
https://www.findagrave.com/memorial/61571178/catherine_schaefer

WILLIAM & KATIE were the parents of:
i. WILBERT HENRY SCHAEFER (1921-2020) WW II Veteran, U.S. Army Air Corps
ii. JAMES G. SCHAEFER (1925-2012) WW II Veteran, U.S. Army Air Corps; and Korean War Veteran, U.S. Air Force
iii. ELEANORE MAE SCHAEFER FLINT (1929-1948):
Wife of ROBERT ELLIS FLINT (1923-) son of IRVING LESTER FLINT (1888-1953) & GERTRUDE GOLDSTEIN (1890-1985), married about 1947. Per her obituary, Eleanore died on 4 March 1948, due to complications following childbirth, of a daughter, Roel Irene Flint. It is unknown what became of Roel Irene and her father, Robert Flint.
https://www.findagrave.com/memorial/61572108/eleanor-mae-flint

31. ELISABETH (ELIZABETH) SCHAEFER Born on 21 December 1871 in McHenry Township, McHenry County, Illinois. Elizabeth died at her home in McHenry, McHenry County, Illinois on 4 November 1966; she was 95. Burial at St. Mary's Catholic Cemetery in McHenry:
https://www.findagrave.com/memorial/68732437/elizabeth_kennebeck
Obituary in McHenry Plaindealer.

On 13 February 1890 when ELISABETH SCHAEFER was 18, she married HEINRICH BERNARD (HENRY) KENNEBECK, son of JOHANN BERNARD KERNEBECK (1807-1883) & ADELHEID HEMLING (1820-1891), at St. John the Baptist Catholic Church in Johnsburg, McHenry County, Illinois. HENRY KENNEBECK was born on 15 January 1865 in Pistakee, McHenry County, Illinois. Henry died at his home in McHenry Township, McHenry County, Illinois on 7 February 1911, following complications while recovering from pneumonia; he was 46. Burial at St. Mary's Catholic Cemetery in McHenry:
https://www.findagrave.com/memorial/49375111/henry_kennebeck
Obituary on memorial and in McHenry Plaindealer, 16 February 1911, Front page.

ELISABETH SCHAEFER AND HENRY KENNEBECK

BACK ROW, LEFT TO RIGHT: ANNA MARGARETHA KENNEBECK (M. HENRY STILLING), HENRY TONYAN, BEST MAN (M. ELIZABETH GERTRUDE ALTHOFF), ANNA "ANNIE" SCHAEFER (M. JOSEPH JUSTEN) AND JOSEPH SCHAEFER (M. ELIZABETH SABEL)

ELISABETH & HENRY were the parents of the following children, including 2 sets of twins:

124. i. NICOLAUS BERNARD "BEN" KENNEBECK (1891-1970)
125. ii. JOHN KENNEBECK (1893-1978)
126. iii. JOSEPH KENNEBECK (1895-infant, Twin of HEINRICH)
127. iv. HEINRICH KENNEBECK (1895-infant, Twin of JOSEPH)
128. v. TERESA "TRACE" KENNEBECK FREUND (1896-1989, Twin of HENRY)
129. vi. HENRY JOSEPH "HENRY" KENNEBECK (1896-1978, Twin of TRACE)
130. vii. ELISABETH KENNEBECK (1898-infant)
131. viii. JOSEPH KENNEBECK (1901-1902)
132. ix. EDWARD JOSEPH (EDWARD) KENNEBECK (1903-1983)
133. x. ARTHUR NICOLAUS "ART" KENNEBECK (1906-1979)
134. xi. MARCELLA KENNEBECK WEINGART (1908-1992)
135. xii. THEODORE KENNEBECK (1910-1911)

124. NICOLAUS BERNARD "BEN" KENNEBECK Born on 20 July 1891 in Pistakee, McHenry County, Illinois. Ben died in McHenry, McHenry County, Illinois on 6 October 1970; he was 79. Burial at St. Mary's Catholic Cemetery in McHenry: https://www.findagrave.com/memorial/58587072/bernard-nicholas-kennebeck

On 4 October 1916 when BEN KENNEBECK was 25, he married CHRISTINE MARIE FREUND, daughter of PETER MARTIN FREUND (1868-1934) & MARIA ANNA MAY (1869-1947), at St.

Mary's Catholic Church in McHenry, McHenry County, Illinois. CHRISTINE MARIE FREUND was born on 29 July 1896 in Spring Grove, McHenry County, Illinois. Christine died in McHenry, McHenry County, Illinois on 15 September 1986; she was 69. Burial at St. Mary's Catholic Cemetery in McHenry: https://www.findagrave.com/memorial/58587026/christina_m_kennebeck

CHRISTINE FREUND & BEN KENNEBECK

BEN & CHRISTINE were the parents of:
i. ELIZABETH LOUISE KENNEBECK (1926-1926)
ii. EARL JOHN KENNEBECK (1929-2008). Earl never married
iii. MARIE KENNEBECK (1934-1934)

125. JOHN KENNEBECK Born on 1 December 1893 in Pistakee, McHenry County, Illinois. John never married. He died in McHenry, McHenry County, Illinois on 19 September 1978; he was 84. Burial at St. Mary's Catholic Cemetery in McHenry: https://www.findagrave.com/memorial/69060723/john_kennebeck

John Kennebeck

126. JOSEPH KENNEBECK Born on 10 June 1895 in Pistakee, McHenry County, Illinois. Joseph was a twin of Heinrich. He died as an infant, date not known. Burial would have been at St. John the Baptist Cemetery in Johnsburg.

127. HEINRICH KENNEBECK Born on 10 June 1895 in Pistakee, McHenry County, Illinois. Heinrich was the twin of Joseph. Heinrich also died while an infant, date not known. Burial would have been at St. John the Baptist Cemetery in Johnsburg.

128. TERESA "TRACE" KENNEBECK Twin sister of Henry Joseph, was born on 23 July 1896 in Pistakee, McHenry County, Illinois. Trace died in Crystal Lake, McHenry County, Illinois on 21 December 1989; she was 93. Burial at St. Mary's Catholic Cemetery in McHenry, McHenry County, Illinois.

On 9 February 1916, when TRACE KENNEBECK was 19, she married PETER ALVIN FREUND, son of JOHN S. FREUND (1861-1938) & HELENA "LENA" MICHELS (1866-1941), at St. Mary's Catholic Church in McHenry, McHenry County, Illinois. PETER FREUND was born on 29 August 1890 in Johnsburg, McHenry County, Illinois. Peter died in McHenry on 23 February

1978; he was 87. Burial at St. Mary's Catholic Cemetery in McHenry:
https://www.findagrave.com/memorial/69060600/peter-a-freund

TRACE KENNEBECK AND PETER FREUND

TRACE & PETER were the parents of:
i. BERNICE ELIZABETH FREUND (1916-2014) (Never Married)
ii. ORVILLE FREUND (1918-2007)

129. HENRY JOSEPH KENNEBECK Twin of Anna Teresa "Trace", was born on 23 July 1896 in Pistakee, McHenry County, Illinois. Henry died in Woodstock, McHenry County, Illinois on 12 October 1976; he was 80. Burial at St. Mary's Catholic Cemetery in McHenry, McHenry County, Illinois:
https://www.findagrave.com/memorial/69834902/henry_joseph_kennebeck

On 23 October 1923, when HENRY JOSEPH KENNEBECK was 27, he married ROSA NIMSGERN, daughter of FRANK NIMSGERN (1874-1922) & CATHERINE SCHAEFER (1877-1942), at St. Peter's Catholic Church in Spring Grove, McHenry County, Illinois. ROSA NIMSGERN was born on 25 February 1902 in Spring Grove. Rosa died in Woodstock, McHenry County, Illinois on 11 August 1983; she was 83. Burial at St. Mary's Catholic Cemetery in McHenry:

https://www.findagrave.com/memorial/69834925/rosa_kennebeck

ROSA NIMSGERN & HENRY KENNEBECK

HENRY & ROSA were the parents of:
i. BERNARD VERNON KENNEBECK ("VERNON" / "KENNY") (1924-2000) WW II Veteran, U.S. Navy
ii. ELVERA MARY KENNEBECK SCHWARTZ (1928-2005)
iii. DAVID JOSEPH KENNEBECK (1945-Living) Vietnam Veteran, U.S. Air Force

"Vern" Kennebeck & Carmela Marangi

Elvera Kennebeck &
William Schwartz

David Kennebeck &
Isabelle Mongeau

130. ELISABETH KENNEBECK Born on 13 July 1898 in Pistakee, McHenry County, Illinois. Elisabeth died as an infant, date not known. Burial location unknown.

131. JOSEPH KENNEBECK Born on 23 March 1901 McHenry, McHenry County, Illinois. Joseph died on 4/5 October 1902 in McHenry. Burial at St. Mary's Catholic Cemetery in McHenry.

132. EDWARD JOSEPH "ED" KENNEBECK Born on 11 May 1903 in McHenry, McHenry County, Illinois. Ed died in McHenry, McHenry County, Illinois on 29 May 1983; he was 80. Burial at St. Mary's Catholic Cemetery in McHenry:
https://www.findagrave.com/memorial/69114700/edward_joseph_kennebeck
Obituary on memorial and in McHenry Plaindealer.

On 3 December 1938, EDWARD KENNEBECK married 1. ADELE PRITCHETT/PRICKETT nee BETHOLD of St. Louis, Missouri. ADELE BETHOLD was born on 11 October 1904 in St. Louis, Missouri. Adele died in Lyons, Cook County, Illinois on 25 February 1952; she was 48. Burial at St. Matthew Cemetery in St. Louis City, Missouri.
Adele was previously married to Thomas Arthur Prickett/Prichett on 4 January 1926 in Snohomish County, Washington:
https://www.findagrave.com/memorial/84163006/adele_e_kennebeck

NOTE: *Ed & Adele had no children.*

On 9 November 1974, when EDWARD KENNEBECK was 71, he married 2. widow ALVINA MARIE GIBBS nee MILLER, daughter of JACOB MILLER (1871-1939) & CATHARINA THELEN (1877-1939). AlVINA MILLER was born on 2 March 1905 in Johnsburg, McHenry County, Illinois. Alvina died in McHenry, McHenry County, Illinois on 3 December 1979; she was 74. Alvina is at rest beside her first husband, RUSSELL

WILLIAM GIBBS (1904-1955), at St. Mary's Catholic Cemetery in McHenry:
https://www.findagrave.com/memorial/84163356/alvina_marie_gibbs_kennebeck

133. ARTHUR NICOLAUS "ART" KENNEBECK Born on 8 January 1906 in McHenry, McHenry County, Illinois. Art died in McHenry on 3 January 1979. Burial at St. Mary's Catholic Cemetery in McHenry:
https://www.findagrave.com/memorial/69060699/arthur_n_kennebeck

On 26 November 1929, when ARTHUR KENNEBECK was 23, he married LOUISE CHAMBERLIN, the adopted daughter of ROLLO GUY CHAMBERLIN (1874-1952) & FANNIE JOSEPHINE MAE DENSMORE (1879-1951), in Chicago, Cook County, Illinois. LOUISE CHAMBERLIN was born on 1 July 1907 in Lake Bluff, Cook County, Illinois, her birth parents are not known. Louise died in McHenry, McHenry County, Illinois on 9 July 1981. Burial at St. Mary's Catholic Cemetery in McHenry:
https://www.findagrave.com/memorial/69060688/louise_kennebeck

ARTHUR & LOUISE were the parents of:
i. GAYLE KENNEBECK GROFF (1930-2014)
    NOTE: Maternal ancestry unknown
ii. LINDA KENNEBECK (1948-1970)
    NOTE: Maternal ancestry unknown

134. MARCELLA KENNEBECK Born on 21 September 1908 in McHenry, McHenry County, Illinois. Marcella died in Crystal Lake, McHenry County, Illinois on 28 June 1992; she was 83. Burial at St. Mary's Catholic Cemetery in McHenry:
https://www.findagrave.com/memorial/69834988/marcella_weingart

On 14 February 1942, when MARCELLA KENNEBECK was 33, she married ALFRED HERBERT WEINGART, son of NICHOLAS SIMON WEINGART (1885-1956) & ANNA MARIA (MARY) WEBER (1886-1959), at St. Mary's Catholic

Church in McHenry, McHenry County, Illinois. ALFRED "AL" WEINGART was born on 17 January 1909 in Griswold Lake, McHenry County, Illinois. Al died in Woodstock, McHenry County, Illinois on 29 July 1978; he was 69. Burial at St. Mary's Catholic Cemetery in McHenry. Marcella & Al had no children. Al Weingart was a World War II Veteran, 101st Airborne, he fought in the Battle of Normandy, he was a member of McHenry Post No. 491 of the American Legion:
https://www.findagrave.com/memorial/69834952/alfred_herbert_weingart

MARCELLA KENNEBECK AND AL WEINGART

135. THEODORE KENNEBECK Born on 22 March 1910 in McHenry, McHenry County, Illinois. Theodore died as an infant, sometime after 7 February 1911. Burial at St. Mary's Catholic Cemetery in McHenry.

32. ANNA "ANNIE" SCHAEFER Born on 19 November 1874 in McHenry Township, McHenry County, Illinois. Annie died in McHenry, McHenry County, Illinois on 1 April 1963; she was 87. Burial at St. Mary's Catholic Cemetery in McHenry: https://www.findagrave.com/memorial/68753026/annie_justen

On 12 January 1893 when ANNIE SCHAEFER was 18, she married JOSEPH HENRY JUSTEN, son of JOHN JOSEPH JUSTEN (1844-1924) & SUSANNA KLAPPERICH (1851-1916), at St. John the Baptist Catholic Church in Johnsburg, McHenry County, Illinois. JOSEPH JUSTEN was born on 26 October 1871 in Johnsburg. Joseph, following an unknown illness of 2 years, died on 22 March 1908 in McHenry, McHenry County, Illinois; he was 36. Burial at St. Mary's Catholic Cemetery in McHenry. Obituary: McHenry Plaindealer, 26 March 1908, Front page. https://www.findagrave.com/memorial/68753000/joseph_h_justen

> *NOTE: Annie never remarried after the death of Joseph.*

ANNIE SCHAEFER AND JOSEPH JUSTEN

ANNIE & JOSEPH were the parents of:
136. i. SUSANNA JUSTEN SCHAEFER (1893-1969)
137. ii. JOHANN R. (JOHN) JUSTEN (1896-1957)
138. iii. ELIZABETH AGNES JUSTEN MILLER (1898-1981)
139. iv. JOSEPH JUSTEN (1900-1902)
140. v. WILLIAM HENRY JUSTEN (1902-1988)
141. vi. FERDINAND JACOB JUSTEN (1904-1910)
142. vii. FRIEDRICH JUSTEN (1905-1905)
143. viii. FRIEDRICH BERNARD JUSTEN (1906-1908)
144. ix. ANNA MARIA JUSTEN (1907-1908)

136. SUSANNA JUSTEN Born on 19 July 1893 in McHenry Township, McHenry County, Illinois. Susanna died in McHenry on 11 November 1969; she was 76. Burial at St. Mary's Catholic Cemetery in McHenry:
https://www.findagrave.com/memorial/68750854/susan_schaefer

On 17 November 1917 when SUSANNA "SUSIE" JUSTEN was 21, she married JOSEPH ALBERT SCHAEFER, son of PETER SCHAEFER (1851-1939) & CATHARINA FRETT (1858-1933), at St. Mary's Catholic Church in McHenry. JOSEPH ALBERT SCHAEFER was born on 8 June 1887 in Chicago, Cook County, Illinois. Joseph died in Woodstock, McHenry County, Illinois on 11 April 1974; he was 86. Burial at St. Mary's Catholic Cemetery in McHenry:
https://www.findagrave.com/memorial/68750828/joseph_albert_schaefer

SUSANNA & JOSEPH were parents of:
i. ELMER JOHN SCHAEFER (1918-2000)
ii. ELEANORE LILLIAN SCHAEFER MILLER (1925-2009)

137. JOHN R. JUSTEN Born on 11 May 1896 in McHenry Township, McHenry County, Illinois. John died in McHenry, McHenry County, Illinois on 12 February 1957; he was 60. Burial at St. Mary's Catholic Cemetery in McHenry:
https://www.findagrave.com/memorial/61263504/john_r_justen

On 5 November 1919 when JOHN JUSTEN was 19 he married ANNA MARIA "EVELYN" LOUISE FREUND, age 16, daughter of FRANK JOSEPH FREUND (1873-1925) & ANNA MAY (1877-1949), at St. Mary's Catholic Church in McHenry, McHenry County, Illinois. EVELYN LOUISE FREUND was born on 15 April 1899 in McHenry, McHenry County, Illinois. Evelyn died in McHenry on 21 August 1980; she was 80. Burial at St. Mary's Catholic Cemetery in McHenry:
https://www.findagrave.com/memorial/61263577/evelyn_justen

JOHN & EVELYN were the parents of:
i. SUSANNA G. (GLADYS) JUSTEN EKHOLM (1920-2008)
ii. EUGENE JAMES JUSTEN (1921-1999)
    WW II and Korean War Veteran, U.S. Air Force
iii. GERALD WILLIAM JUSTEN (1923-1951)
    Casualty of Korean War
iv. JOHN J. (JACK) JUSTEN (1932-2014) WW II Veteran, U.S. Army

138. ELIZABETH AGNES "LIZZIE" JUSTEN Born on 10 April 1898 in McHenry Township, McHenry County, Illinois. Elizabeth died in Crystal Lake, McHenry County, Illinois on 27 December 1981; she was 83. Burial at St. Mary's Catholic Cemetery in McHenry:
https://www.findagrave.com/memorial/69836294/elizabeth_a_miller

On 6 September 1916, when ELIZABETH JUSTEN was 17, she married ANTHONY JACOB "TONY" MILLER, age 22, son of FRANK MILLER (1848-1931) & KATHARINA KERLING (1852-1927), at St. John the Baptist Catholic Church in Johnsburg, McHenry County, Illinois. ANTHONY JACOB MILLER was born on 25 March 1894 in Johnsburg, McHenry County, Illinois. Anthony died at Woodstock Hospital in Woodstock, McHenry County, Illinois on 3 October 1961; he was 67. Burial at St. Mary's Catholic Cemetery in McHenry:
https://www.findagrave.com/memorial/69836261/anthony_j_miller
Obituary in McHenry Plaindealer, 5 October 1961, page 3.

ELIZABETH & ANTHONY were the parents of:
i. RICHARD JOHN MILLER (1917-1984)
ii. SARAH S. MILLER GROELL (1921-2002)
iii. ESTELLE E. MILLER ENGELS (1923-2008)

139. JOSEPH JUSTEN Born on 17 July 1900 in McHenry Township, McHenry County, Illinois. Joseph died on 17 May 1902 in McHenry Township. Burial at St. Mary's Catholic Cemetery in McHenry.

140. WILLIAM HENRY JUSTEN Born on 29 August 1902 in McHenry Township, McHenry County, Illinois. William died in Elgin, Kane County, Illinois on 4 October 1988; he was 85. Burial at Dundee Township Cemetery in East Dundee, Kane County, Illinois:
https://www.findagrave.com/memorial/26497807/william_henry_justen

On 12 February 1931, when WILLIAM JUSTEN was 29, he married CLARA MYRTLE ERLANDSON, daughter of CAPTAIN, JOHN ERLANDSON (1854-1903) & ANNIE

ANDERSON (1858-1937), at St. Mary's Catholic Church in McHenry. CLARA MYRTLE ERLANDSON was born in Kane County, Illinois in January 1894. Clara died in 1973; she was 79. Burial at Dundee Township Cemetery in East Dundee, Kane County, Illinois:
https://www.findagrave.com/memorial/26497794/clara_myrtle_justen

WILLIAM & CLARA had no known children

141. FERDINAND JACOB JUSTEN Born on 3 October 1904 in McHenry Township, McHenry County, Illinois. Ferdinand died at the age of 6 years in McHenry on 14 February 1910. Burial at St. Mary's Catholic Cemetery in McHenry, McHenry County, Illinois.

142. FRIEDRICH (FRED) JUSTEN Born on 3 September 1905 in McHenry Township, McHenry County, Illinois, died on 12 October 1905. Burial at St. Mary's Catholic Cemetery, McHenry.

143. FRIEDRICH BERNARD (FRED) JUSTEN Born on 21/27 September 1906 in McHenry Township, McHenry County, Illinois, died in McHenry on 6 May 1908. Burial at St. Mary's Catholic Cemetery, McHenry.

144. ANNA MARIA JUSTEN Born on 21 October 1907 in McHenry Township, McHenry County, Illinois. Burial at St. Mary's Catholic Cemetery, McHenry.

> **NOTE**: St. Mary Catholic Church records document her date of death as "17 November 1908" and burial as "22 November 1908". Transcribed County Death Certificate documents her date of death as "17 OCTOBER 1908", 11 months 28 days, following an illness of 8 days, buried on "19 October 1908":
> https://www.findagrave.com/memorial/68818632/anna_maria_justen

33. MATHIAS SCHAEFER Born on 5 July 1877 in McHenry Township, McHenry County, Illinois, died on 1 August 1877 in McHenry Township, McHenry County, Illinois. Burial at St. John the Baptist Cemetery in Johnsburg, McHenry County, Illinois.

34. MICHAEL SCHAEFER Born on 24 September 1881 in McHenry Township, McHenry County, Illinois. His birth and baptism were recorded at St. Patrick's Catholic Church in McHenry. When Michael died is unknown.

Descendants of JACOB SCHMITT & ANNA GOEDERT through their daughter Gertrud (Nikolaus Schaefer): 10 Grandchildren (Bold Black)
42 Great-grandchildren (Fuchsia)
71 2x Great-grandchildren (Teal)

Chapter V

NICHOLAS SCHMITT

5. NICHOLAS SCHMITT Born on 7 October 1841 in Johnsburg, McHenry County, Illinois. NICHOLAS SCHMITT was the first child born in Johnsburg to immigrant parents who settled in what became Johnsburg, McHenry County, Illinois. Nicholas's father JACOB SCHMITT was one of three founders of Johnsburg in August 1841. NICHOLAS SCHMITT died at the home of his son JOHN SCHMITT in Jamestown, Stutsman County, North Dakota on 23 August 1929. Burial on 27 August 1929 in the Schmitt family plot at Japanese Martyrs Catholic Cemetery in Leavenworth, Brown County, Minnesota:
https://www.findagrave.com/memorial/130619790/nicholas-schmitt

Nicholas Schmitt was a Veteran of the Civil War, Co. E 9th Regiment Illinois Volunteer Cavalry. His record shows he mustered in on 13 February 1864, mustered out 31 October 1865. During his time in service he would have participated in the following expeditions: Expedition from Eastport to Russellville, Alabama February 19-28, 1865. Tuscumbia February 20. Duty at Huntsville and Florence, Alabama, Eastport, Mississippi, and Gravelly Springs, Alabama, until June. Moved to Luka, Mississippi, June 23, thence to Decatur, Alabama; then July 4 to

Montgomery and Selma, Alabama; thence to Gainesville on August 20. Duty in District of Montgomery, Alabama, until October. Mustered out at Selma, Alabama, on 31 October 1865. Regiment lost during service: 1 Officer, 45 Enlisted men killed and mortally wounded, 6 Officers and 241 Enlisted men by disease. Total: 293.

Illinois State Archives Illinois Civil War Detail Report:

Name: SMITT, NICHOLAS; Rank: Private; Company: E; Unit: 9th Regiment Illinois Cavalry; Residence: McHenry, McHenry County, Illinois; Age: 23; Height: 5' 9 1/2"; Hair: Brown; Eyes: Grey; Complexion: Light; Marital Status: [Married]; Occupation: Farmer; Nativity: Illinois; Service Record; Joined: 13 February 1865; Joined: Marengo, McHenry County, Illinois; Joined By: Captain Coon; Period: 1 Year; Muster In: 14 February 1865; Muster In At: Marengo, McHenry County, Illinois; Muster In By: [Blank]; Muster Out: 31 October 1865; Muster Out: Selma, Alabama; Muster Out By: Lieutenant Hosner.

On 20 November 1862 NICHOLAS SCHMITT married MARIA MEILER, daughter of ANTON MEILER (1806-1872) & 1. ELI(S)ZABETH PREUSS (1818-1904), at St. John the Baptist Catholic Church in Johnsburg, McHenry County, Illinois. MARIA MEILER was born on 17 March 1841 in Weiler, Dist. Mayen, Rhineland, Prussia. MARIA SCHMITT died in Leavenworth, Mulligan Twp., Brown County, Minnesota on 6 December 1910. Burial on 9 December 1910 in the Schmitt family plot at Japanese Martyrs Catholic Cemetery in Leavenworth, Brown County, Minnesota:

https://www.findagrave.com/memorial/130619921/marie-schmitt

NICHOLAS SCHMITT & MARIA MEILER

(Transcribed by MCIGS in 1985)
Early Records of St. John the Baptist Catholic Church
Johnsburg, McHenry Co., Illinois
Volume I: 1852-1868
Nicolaus SCHMITT & Maria MEILER
m 20 Nov 1862
Witnesses: Bernhard MEILER & Friedrich SCHMITT.

NICHOLAS & MARIA were the parents of the following children. Births & baptisms of their first five children born in Johnsburg, McHenry County, Illinois were recorded at St. John the Baptist Catholic Church:

35. i. ANTON SCHMITT (1863-1931)
36. ii. ELIZABETH SCHMITT LENT (1864-1937)
37. iii. HELENA SCHMITT BUNGER (1866-1968)
38. iv. NICOLAUS JOSEPH SCHMITT (1867-1960)
39. v. GERTRUDE SCHMITT SCOTT (1869-bet 1950 & 1968)
40. vi. KATHERINE SCHMITT TORREY (1870-1967)
41. vii. JOHN G. SCHMITT (1872-1975)
42. viii. JOSEPH SCHMITT (1874-1964)
43. ix. MATHIAS PETER SCHMITT (1876-1876)

44. x.   MARY K. SCHMITT ARNOLDI (1877-1958)
45. xi. ROSALIA SCHMITT ECKERT-HICKEL (1879-1957)
46. xii. BERTHA K. SCHMITT FITZPATRICK (1880-1953)
47. xiii. CHARLES SCHMITT (1882-1896)
48. xiv. FRANK J. SCHMITT (1883-1969)
49. xv. WILLIAM HENRY SCHMITT (1887-1914)

Descendants of JACOB SCHMITT & ANNA GOEDERT
Grandchildren (Bold Black)
Great-grandchildren (Fuchsia)
2x Great-grandchildren (Teal)

Nicholas and Maria left Johnsburg, McHenry County, Illinois and moved on to Minnesota, sometime after the birth of their fifth child Gertrude Schmitt, born in Johnsburg, McHenry County, Illinois on 20 August 1869. Their next child, Katherine Schmitt, was born on 15 October 1870 at New Ulm, Mulligan Township, Brown County, Minnesota. Per his obituary, his brother Peter Schmitt accompanied the family to Minnesota.

Bismarck Tribune, Jamestown, North Dakota, August 26, 1929:

> *"Nicholas Schmitt, 90-year-old Civil War Veteran, died at his home here at 1:30 o'clock Sunday morning after an illness of four weeks. Funeral services will be conducted at 9:30 o'clock Tuesday morning from St. James Catholic Church and burial will be made at Comfrey, Minnesota. Enlisting in the Illinois Volunteer Cavalry on February 13, 1864 [1865], he distinguished himself in the Civil War and drew his honorable discharge on October 31, 1865. He was a member of the Fort Seward Post, Grand Army of the Republic. In 1870, Mr. Schmitt, with a brother, drove by ox team from near Chicago to New Ulm, Minnesota where they took up homesteads. He was a farmer all his life except the time he lived in Jamestown. Five sons, five daughters, 27 grandchildren and 15 great-grandchildren survive."*

35. ANTON (ANTHONY) SCHMITT Born on 8 August 1863 in Johnsburg, McHenry County, Illinois. Anthony never married, he died in Stanton, Mercer County, North Dakota or in Williams County, North Dakota, on 23 May 1931. Burial at Highland Cemetery in Ray, Williams County, North Dakota:
https://www.findagrave.com/memorial/233036468/anthony-schmitt

36. ELIZABETH SCHMITT Born on 24 December 1864 in Johnsburg, McHenry County, Illinois. Elizabeth may have died in Springfield, Brown County, Minnesota on 21 November 1937. Burial location unknown.

On 28 August 1884 ELIZABETH SCHMITT married Dr. ADDISON LENT, son of ROBERT HOWARD LENT (1821-1888) & SARAH BARTLETT (abt 1821-aft 27 January 1888), in New Ulm, Brown County, Minnesota. ADDISON LENT, a physician, was born on 24 May 1853 in Albany, Albany County, New York. Addison died in Doyon, Ramsey County, North Dakota, on 22 February 1916. Burial at Doyon Cemetery in Doyon, Ramsey County, North Dakota:
https://www.findagrave.com/memorial/255236284/addison_lent

ELIZABETH & ADDISON were the parents of:
145. i. HENRY EDWARD LENT (1885-1958)
146. ii. LOTTIE LILLIAN LENT ROWE (1886-1957)

145. HENRY EDWARD LENT Born on 9 January 1885 in Springfield, Brown County, Minnesota. Henry died in Omro, Winnebago County, Wisconsin on 28 October 1958. Burial at Omro Cemetery in Omro:
https://www.findagrave.com/memorial/144048603/henry_edward_lent

On 26 May 1914 HENRY EDWARD LENT married WILHELMINA "MINNIE" KAEHLER, daughter of CARL KAEHLER (1871-1914) & PAULINE SCHILLER (1873-1959), in New Ulm, Brown County, Minnesota. WILHELMINA KAEHLER was born on 7 September 1887 in Springfield, Greene County, Missouri. Wilhelmina died in Saint Cloud, Stearns County, Minnesota, on 21 December 1957. Burial at Benton County Cemetery in Sauk Rapids, Benton County, Minnesota.

NOTE: Marriage ended in divorce.

New Ulm Review newspaper, Wednesday 16 May 1917, Wilhelmina Lent vs Henry E. Lent. She married 2. CHARLES ARTHUR SWANSON (1895-1981), on 9 May 1918 in Springfield, Brown County, Minnesota.
https://www.findagrave.com/memorial/213994910/wilhelmina_louise_anna_swanson

HENRY & Wilhelmina were the parents of:

i. LELAND CHARLES HENRY LENT (1914-1946)
   https://www.findagrave.com/memorial/163375074/leland_charles_henry_lent

146. **LOTTIE LILLIAN LENT** Born on 12 March 1886 in Springfield, Brown County, Minnesota. Per Find A Grave memorial, Lottie died in Oklahoma City, Oklahoma in 1957. Burial at Memorial Park Cemetery in Oklahoma City:
https://www.findagrave.com/memorial/53895202/lottie_lillian_rowe

On 14 August 1906, LOTTIE LILLIAN LENT married DELBERT LESTER ROWE, son of SERGT. WILLIAM HENRY ROWE (1840-1922) & MARY PERMELIA BARKER (1847-1940), in Springfield, Brown County, Minnesota. DELBERT LESTER

ROWE was born on 3 September 1880 in Olwein, Fayette County, Iowa. Delbert died in Oklahoma City, Oklahoma in 1957. Burial at Memorial Park Cemetery in Oklahoma City.

LOTTIE & DELBERT were the parents of:
i.   RUSSELL DELBERT ROWE (1907-1928)
ii. WARREN B. ROWE (1916-1965)
iii. ELIZABETH J. "BETTY" ROWE ALLISON (JOHN) (1922-)

37. HELENA SCHMITT Born on 16 September 1866 in Johnsburg, McHenry County, Illinois. Helena died in Edgeley, LaMoure County, North Dakota on 12 August 1968. She was 101, a Centenarian. Burial at Calvary Cemetery in Jamestown, Stutsman County, North Dakota:
https://www.findagrave.com/memorial/123478367/helena-bunger

On 7 July 1899 HELENA SCHMITT married WILLIAM BUNGER, son of HENRY BUNGER (1833-1916) & BERNARDINE "DINA" LAH (1839-1928), in Leavenworth, Brown County, Minnesota. WILLIAM BUNGER was born on 3 April 1867 in Cincinnati, Hamilton County, Ohio. William died in Santa Ana, Orange County, California on 24 August 1926. Burial at Fairhaven Memorial Park in Santa Ana:
https://www.findagrave.com/memorial/116011568/william_bunger

HELENA & WILLIAM had no known children.

38. NICHOLAS JOSEPH SCHMITT Born on 20 December 1867 in Johnsburg, McHenry County, Illinois. Nicholas never married. He died in Jamestown, Stutsman County, North Dakota on 3 March 1960. Burial at Calvary Cemetery in Jamestown.

NICHOLAS JOSEPH SCHMITT

39. GERTRUDE SCHMITT Born on 20 August 1869 in Johnsburg, McHenry County, Illinois. Gertrude likely died in Baltimore, Baltimore County, Maryland. She died between May 1950 and August 1968. In the 1920, 1930, 1940 and 1950 Census, Gertrude is living with her daughter Hazell and son-in-law, ROBERT LUTHER EIRICH (1891-1987), in Baltimore City, Maryland.

On 22 July 1888 GERTRUDE SCHMITT married CHARLES WILLIAM SCOTT, son of CHARLES A. SCOTT (1821-1900) & LUCINDA S. RICHARDSON (abt 1827-1898), in Ramsey, Brown County, Minnesota. CHARLES SCOTT was born on 20 August 1869 in Mexico, Oxford County, Maine. Charles died in Baltimore, Maryland some time after the 1910 Census and before the 1920 Census. Date of Death, burial location are unknown.

GERTRUDE & CHARLES were the parents of:
147. i.   HENRY CHARLES SCOTT (1892-1895)
148. ii. HAZELL JANE SCOTT EIRICH (1893-1977)

147. HENRY CHARLES SCOTT Born about 1892 in Burnstown Twp., Brown County, Minnesota. Henry died in November 1895 in Burnstown Twp., Brown County, Minnesota. Burial at Springfield Cemetery in Springfield, Brown County, Minnesota.

148. HAZELL I. SCOTT Born on 18 September 1893 in Burnstown Twp., Brown County, Minnesota. Hazell died in St. Michaels, Talbot County, Maryland on 11 December 1977. Burial at Christ Church Episcopal Cemetery in Saint Michaels, Talbot County, Maryland:
https://www.findagrave.com/memorial/218584540/hazell-i-eirich

On 4 April 1920 HAZELL SCOTT married ROBERT LUTHER EIRICH, son of REV. RICHARD HENRY CHRISTIAN EIRICH (1852-1929) & ELIZABETH BARBARA NICHOL (1854-1926). ROBERT LUTHER EIRICH was born on 1 December 1891 in Hamlin, Monroe County, New York. Robert died in St. Michaels, Talbot County, Maryland on 30 May 1987. Burial at Christ Church Episcopal Cemetery in Saint Michaels, Talbot County, Maryland:
https://www.findagrave.com/memorial/218584617/robert-l-eirich

HAZELL & ROBERT had no known children, per 1930 and 1940 Census records.

40. KATHERINE "KATE" SCHMITT Born on 15 October 1870 in Mulligan Twp., Brown County, Minnesota. Kate died in Eugene, Lane County, Oregon on 23 March 1967. Burial at Sunset Hills Cemetery in Eugene:
https://www.findagrave.com/memorial/124604033/katherine-torrey

On 2 January 1889 KATE SCHMITT married ERVIN DeWITT TORREY, son of JOHN ALVIN TORREY (abt 1836-1913) & SARAH A. GREEN (1846-1933), in New Ulm, Brown County,

Minnesota. ERVIN DEWITT TORREY was born on 4 May 1865 in Goodhue County, Minnesota. Ervin died in Eldridge, Stutsman County, North Dakota in 1946. Burial at Highland Home Cemetery in Jamestown, Stutsman County, North Dakota:
https://www.findagrave.com/memorial/177119700/ervin_dewitt_torrey

KATE SCHMITT & ERVIN DEWITT TORREY

KATE & ERVIN were the parents of:

149. i. ROY LESLIE TORREY (1890-1967)
150. ii. RALPH RENVILLE TORREY (1893-1971) WW I Veteran

149. ROY LESLIE TORREY Born on 15 March 1890 in Brown County, Minnesota. Roy died in Jamestown, Stutsman County, North Dakota in 14 June 1967. Burial at Calvary Cemetery in Jamestown:
https://www.findagrave.com/memorial/117524731/roy_leslie_torrey

On 15 December 1910, ROY LESLIE TORREY married 1. KATHERINE MARY O'DELL, daughter of ISAAC LACEY O'DELL (1861-1940) & "ALCIE" ELIZABETH PHELPS

(1859-1938), in Jamestown, Stutsman County, North Dakota. KATHERINE MARY O'DELL was born on 8 April 1888 in Montgomery County, Indiana. Katherine died in Lakota, Nelson County, North Dakota on 31 January 1914. Burial at Highland Home Cemetery in Jamestown, Stutsman County, North Dakota: https://www.findagrave.com/memorial/177122606/katherine_torrey

ROY & 1. KATHERINE O'DELL were the parents of a daughter:
i. PEARL EVANGELINE TORREY LUSK (1911-1998)
https://www.findagrave.com/memorial/124604076/pearl-evangeline-lusk

On 7 March 1916, ROY LESLIE TORREY married 2. CHRISTINE SONNEK, daughter of ANDREW SONNEK (1818-1892) & CATHERINE VELOSKE/VELOSKI/WIELOWSKI (1846-1919), in Stutsman County, North Dakota. CHRISTINE SONNEK was born on 11 February 1885 in Minnesota Lake Township, Fairbault County, Minnesota. Christine died in Jamestown, Stutsman County, North Dakota on 25 March 1981. Burial at Calvary Cemetery in Jamestown:
https://www.findagrave.com/memorial/117583968/christine_torrey

ROY & 2. CHRISTINE SONNEK were the parents of:
i. CLIFFORD PAUL TORREY (1917-1999) WW II Veteran, Captain, U. S. Army:
https://www.findagrave.com/memorial/1259464/clifford_paul_torrey
ii. MARJORIE TORREY LUKANITSCH (1919-2009) WW II Veteran, CPL U. S. Marine Corps:
https://www.findagrave.com/memorial/106697439/lorraine_k_kiernan
iii. LORRAINE K. TORREY KIERNAN (1920-2013)

WW II Veteran, PFC U. S. Marine Corps:
https://www.findagrave.com/memorial/106697439/lorraine_k_kiernan

iv. ELEANOR A. TORREY (1922-1999)
WW II & Korean War Veteran, DK1 U. S. Navy:
https://www.findagrave.com/memorial/177126944/eleanor_torrey

v. ROBERT TORREY (1925-2006) WW II Veteran, B3 U. S. Navy:
https://www.findagrave.com/memorial/177128396/robert_torrey

vi. GENE IRVING TORREY (1927-2008) Korean War, Veteran, PFC U. S. Army:
https://www.findagrave.com/memorial/43479992/gene_i_torrey

150. RALPH RENVILLE TORREY Born on 23 October 1893 in Brown County, Minnesota. Ralph died in San Diego, San Diego County, California on 19 September 1971. Burial at Greenwood Memorial Park in San Diego. WW I Veteran, CMM, U. S. Navy. https://www.findagrave.com/memorial/187386321/ralph_renville_torrey

On 19 December 1914, RALPH RENVILLE TORREY married LOIS C. O'BRIEN in Blue Earth, Minnesota. This marriage ended in divorce, no known children from this marriage.

After 11 January 1920 and, before 4 April 1930, RALPH RENVILLE TORREY married 2. ELINOR O. NN, born about 1906 in Nebraska, no known children from this marriage.

After 11 June 1940, RALPH RENVILLE TORREY married 3. SUSAN MABLE GEREN nee ROBERTS, daughter of ELIAS JASPER "E. J. " ROBERTS (1851-1940) & MARY JANE "MOLLY"

DeSHANZER (1875-1935). Susan was born on 14 July 1898 in Choctaw, Oklahoma County, Oklahoma. Susan died in San Diego County, California on 24 December 1989. Burial at Greenwood Memorial Park in San Diego:
https://www. findagrave. com/memorial/187442338/susan-mable-torrey

41. **JOHN G. SCHMITT** Born on 12 June 1872 in Mulligan Twp., Brown County, Minnesota. John died in Jamestown, Stutsman County, North Dakota on 9 October 1975; he was 103, a Centenarian. Burial at Highland Home Cemetery in Jamestown. JOHN G. SCHMITT was the last surviving child (of 15) born to NICHOLAS SCHMITT & MARIA MEILER.
https://www. findagrave. com/memorial/140844875/john_g_schmitt

JAMESTOWN SUN, Friday 10 October 1975, page 2:

> "Born June 12, 1872, in Brown County, Minnesota, Mr. Schmitt was the son of Mr. and Mrs. Nicholas Schmitt. He attended school in Minnesota and farmed for a time with his parents. In 1902 he came to North Dakota with his brother, Joe, and they settled in Bloom Township where they farmed. He married Rosamond Haskin on September 16, 1913, at Moorhead, Minnesota, and they made their home in Jamestown where Mr. Schmitt was employed with the Northern Pacific Railway in the Freight House. Following his retirement from the railway in 1942, he was employed as a custodian at St. John's Lutheran Church until 1959. Since 1962, he had made his home here with his son-in-law and daughter, Mr. and Mrs. Thomas J. Hayes. His wife died January 1, 1963. Mr. Schmitt was a member of St. John's Lutheran Church and the Brotherhood of Railway Clerks. He is survived by one daughter, Mrs. Thomas J. Hayes (Margaret), Jamestown; and two grandchildren, Mrs. Tom Lindscheid (Linda), Arlington, Virginia; and Mrs. John Bryant (Noreen), Malani, Hawaii. Mr. Schmitt was the last of 14 children in his family."

On 16 September 1913, JOHN SCHMITT married ROSAMOND (ROSA) HASKIN, daughter of GRANVILLE HASKIN (1867-1951) & LAURA ANN HARPER (1874-1961), in Moorhead,

Clay County, Minnesota. ROSA HASKIN was born on 29 September 1884 in Wells, Fairbault County, Minnesota. Rosa died in Jamestown, Stutsman County, North Dakota on 1 January 1963. Burial at Highland Home Cemetery in Jamestown:
https://www.findagrave.com/memorial/140845024/rosamond_a_schmit

JOHN & ROSA were the parents of a daughter:
151. i. MARGARET ANN SCHMITT HAYES (1918-2003) Obituary:

> *"MARGARET ANN SCHMITT was born on 16 April 1918 in Jamestown, Stutsman County, North Dakota. Margaret died in Rockville, Montgomery County, Maryland on 23 May 2003; Margaret was survived by two daughters and sons-in-law, Linda (Terry) Bathen of Annandale, Virginia and Reen (Bill) Lyddane of Annandale, Virginia; three grandchildren, Alexis Wirtz and Billy and Erin Lyddane. She was 84. Margaret was survived by two daughters and sons-in-law, Linda (Terry) Bathen of Annandale, Virginia and Reen (Bill) Lyddane of Annandale, Virginia; three grandchildren, Alexis Wirtz and Billy and Erin Lyddane. Burial at Calvary Cemetery in Jamestown, Stutsman County, North Dakota":*
> https://www.findagrave.com/memorial/115481712/margaret_ann_hayes

On 17 July 1944, MARGARET ANN SCHMITT married THOMAS JAMES HAYES, son of STEPHEN THOMAS HAYES (1886-1961) & IRMA ARVILLA DANCY (1887-1922), in Missoula, Missoula County, Montana. THOMAS HAYES was born 23 October 1912 in Duluth, St. Louis County, Minnesota. Thomas died in Jamestown, Stutsman County, North Dakota on 14 October 1996. Burial at Calvary Cemetery in Jamestown, Stutsman County, North Dakota.

MARGARET & THOMAS were the parents of:

i. LINDA HAYES BATHEN (TERRY)
  ii. NOREEN HAYES LYDDANE (BILL)

42. JOSEPH SCHMITT Born on 20 June 1874 in Mulligan Twp., Brown County, Minnesota. Joseph died in Jamestown, Stutsman County, North Dakota on 22 November 1964. Burial at Calvary Cemetery in Jamestown:
https://www.findagrave.com/memorial/123671132/joseph_schmitt

JAMESTOWN SUN, Monday 23 November 1964, page 4:

> "Born June 20, 1874, in Brown County, Minnesota, Mr. Schmitt was the son of Mr. and Mrs. Nicholas Schmitt. He attended school in Brown County and farmed there for a time. His marriage to Emma Arnoldi took place September 22, 1896, at Leavenworth, Minnesota, and they resided in Brown County until moving to Bloom Township, North Dakota in 1903, where Mr. Schmitt had resided since. Mrs. Schmitt died March 4, 1948. Mr. Schmitt was a member of St. James Catholic Church, a life member of B. P. O. Elks 995, and member of Modern Woodmen Lodge. He was a former director of Bloom Oil Co., a Bloom Township Supervisor, served as school board member for many years, past President of the Bloom Elevator, former Director of both the James River Valley Insurance Co., and Bloom Telephone Co. He is survived by four children, Mrs. Verna Hertzfeldt, Miss Elsie Schmitt and Lowell Schmitt, Jamestown; and Mrs. Evata Murphy, Edgeley; six grandchildren; and one great-grandchild; two brothers, John Schmitt, Jamestown and Frank Schmitt, St. Paul, Minnesota; two sisters, Mrs. Katherine Torrey, Eugene, Oregon, and Mrs. Lena Bunger, Edgeley. He was preceded in death by his wife; a son, Emery, in 1943, and 10 brothers and sisters."

On 22 September 1896, JOSEPH SCHMITT married EMMA ARNOLDI, daughter of MICHAEL ARNOLDI (1826-1901) & ANNA VATOR or "WETOR" (1836-1915), in Leavenworth, Brown County, Minnesota. EMMA ARNOLDI was born on 5 May 1878 in New Ulm, Brown County, Minnesota. Emma died in Jamestown, Stutsman County, North Dakota on 4 March 1948.

Obituary in **JAMESTOWN SUN, Friday 5 March 1948, page 1**:

> "Mrs. Schmitt was born in New Ulm, Brown County, Minnesota, May 5, 1878. She attended school in Brown County. Mrs. Schmitt's parents were living at New Ulm when the Indian massacre took place. Miss Emma Arnoldi and Mr. Schmitt were married in Leavenworth, Minnesota, September 22, 1896. They lived in Brown County until coming to Bloom Township in 1903. They have made their home there since. Mrs. Schmitt has been ill for several years. They are the parents of five children. Mrs. Schmitt was a member of St. James Catholic Church and was active in community life. Survivors are her husband and the following sons and daughters: Mrs. Otto Hertzfeldt and Lowell Schmitt, Bloom Township; Elsie, Jamestown; Mrs. K. Murphy, Edgeley; a sister, Mrs. Anton Schmitz, New Ulm, Minnesota; a brother, Michael Arnoldi, Sanborn, Minnesota. Mr. Arnoldi visited here with his sister last fall. Three granddaughters also survive. A son, Emery, died in 1943."

Burial at Calvary Cemetery in Jamestown:
https://www.findagrave.com/memorial/123671134/emma_schmitt

Joseph and Emma celebrated their Golden Anniversary in September 1946.

JOSEPH & EMMA were the parents of:
- 152. i. VERNA MARIE SCHMITT HERTZFELDT (1898-1977)
- 153. ii. ELSIE V. SCHMITT (1899-1984) Never married
- 154. iii. EMERY NICHOLAS SCHMITT (1904-1943) Never married
- 155. iv. EVATA MARIE SCHMITT MURPHY (1909-1996)
- 156. v. LOWELL MEILER SCHMITT (1916-1993)

152. VERNA MARIA SCHMITT Born on 19 February 1898 in Springfield, Brown County, Minnesota. Verna died in Jamestown, Stutsman County, North Dakota on 23 August 1977. Burial at Calvary Cemetery, Jamestown.

On 10 October 1934, VERNA SCHMITT married OTTO M. HERTZFELDT, son of CHARLES HERTZFELDT (1865-1952) &

AUGUSTE MATHILDE C. THEURER (1866-1912), at St. James Catholic Church in Jamestown, Stutsman County, North Dakota. OTTO HERTZFELDT was born on 31 October 1894 in Arcadia, Trempeleu County, Wisconsin. Otto died in Jamestown on 12 September 1962. Burial at Calvary Cemetery, Jamestown.

VERNA & OTTO had no known children.

153. **ELSIE VERNIA SCHMITT** Born on 13 May 1899 in Springfield, Brown County, Minnesota. Elsie never married. She died in Jamestown, Stutsman County, North Dakota on 3 March 1984. Burial at Calvary Cemetery in Jamestown.

> *"Elsie Schmitt graduated from St. John's Academy in Jamestown. She graduated from Valley City State Teacher's College and taught school in Bloom and Homer Townships and at Enderlin Public School. She was later employed by Otter Tail Power Company in Jamestown. She was a member of St. James Catholic Church, St. James Circle and St. James Tabernacle Society and did volunteer work for the church for 25 years."*

154. **EMERY NICHOLAS SCHMITT** Born on 29 April 1904 in Bloom Township, Stutsman County, North Dakota. Emery N. Schmitt graduated from the Hanson Auto and Tractor School at Fargo, North Dakota. He was one of the prominent farmers in Bloom Township. Emery never married. He died in Jamestown, Stutsman County, North Dakota on 30 October 1943. Burial at Calvary Cemetery in Jamestown.

155. **EVATA MARIE SCHMITT** Born on 28 October 1909 in Jamestown, Stutsman County, North Dakota. Evata died in Dubuque, Dubuque County, Iowa on 28 December 1996. Burial at Mount Calvary Cemetery in Edgeley, LaMoure County, North Dakota.
https://www.findagrave.com/memorial/140847633/evata_marie_murphy

On 11 November 1938, EVATA SCHMITT married WILLIAM

KIMBALL "KIM" MURPHY, son of WILLIAM JAMES MURPHY (1875-1949) & HANNAH KIMBALL (1869-1950), in Jamestown, Stutsman County, North Dakota. WILLIAM KIMBALL MURPHY was born on 8 November 1906 in Ferry Township, Grand Forks County, North Dakota. William died in St. Cloud, Stearns County, Minnesota on 2 November 1961. Burial at Mount Calvary Cemetery in Edgeley, LaMoure County, North Dakota.

EVATA & WILLIAM were the parents of:
 i. THERESA MURPHY CICCIARELLI (1940-)
 ii. MONICA MURPHY CODER (1941-)
 iii. MARY MURPHY HANNITY (abt. 1947-)

156. LOWELL MEILER SCHMITT Born on 7 May 1916 in Jamestown, Stutsman County, North Dakota.

> **NOTE**: *His middle name, MEILER, was the maiden name of his paternal grandmother, Maria (nee MEILER) SCHMITT.*

Lowell died in Jamestown on 3 June 1993. Burial at Calvary Cemetery in Jamestown. Obituary in Jamestown Sun, Saturday 5 June 1883, page 3.
https://www.findagrave.com/memorial/123671098/lowell-meiler-schmitt

On 30 October 1950, LOWELL SCHMITT married MARGARET L. KVISLEN, daughter of ADOLPH KVISLEN (1891-1962) & EDNA AMUNDSON (1895-1981), in Stutsman County, North Dakota. MARGARET KVISLEN was born on 23 March 1916 in Sanborn, Brown County, North Dakota. Margaret died in Jamestown, Stutsman County, North Dakota on 27 June 2007. Burial at Calvary Cemetery in Jamestown.

LOWELL & MARGARET were the parents of:
 i. JOSEPH M. SCHMITT
 ii. JULIE ANN SCHMITT (1953-1953)

iii. JOY SCHMITT McBEAIN
iv. JEFFERY SCHMITT
v. INFANT DAUGHTER SCHMITT (1958-1958)

43. MATHIAS PETER SCHMITT Born on 11 May 1876 in Mulligan Twp., Brown County, Minnesota. Mathias died on 14 June/July 1876 in Mulligan Twp. Burial on the SCHMITT family farm, per Marjorie Beiser (Frederick) nee Budach, a granddaughter of Mary SCHMITT (Peter ARNOLDI).

44. MARY KATHERINE SCHMITT Born on 6 May 1877 in Mulligan Twp., Brown County, Minnesota. Mary Katherine died in Breckenridge, Wilkin County, Minnesota on 23 September 1958; she was 81. Burial at Graceville Cemetery in Graceville Township, Big Stone County, Minnesota.
https://www.findagrave.com/memorial/241609880/mary_katherine_arnoldi

On 22 September 1896, MARY KATHERINE SCHMITT married PETER MATHEW ARNOLDI, son of MICHAEL ARNOLDI (1826-1901) & ANNA VATNOR (1836-1915), in Leavenworth, Brown County, Minnesota. PETER MATHEW ARNOLDI was born on 8 November 1868 in New Ulm, Brown County, Minnesota. Peter died in Tara Twp., Traverse County, Minnesota on 29 May 1927. Burial at Graceville Consolidated Cemetery in Graceville, Big Stone County, Minnesota.

PETER ARNOLDI &
MARY SCHMITT

MARY KATHERINE & PETER were the parents of:
157. i.　ORA RAYFIELD ARNOLDI (1897-1966)
158. ii.　JESSIE VIOLA ARNOLDI BILLIET (1898-1994)
159. iii.　ELRA LEO ARNOLDI (1900-1971) WW II Veteran, U. S. Army Air Forces
160. iv.　VERONICA ESTHER "VERA" ARNOLDI SMITH (1902-1995)
161. v.　MAGDALENA UNA ARNOLDI (1905-1999)
162. vi.　ANGELINE KATHERINE ARNOLDI BUDACH-PELZINSKI (1906-1997)
163. vii.　ELIZABETH ARNOLDI (1908-1908)
164. viii.　WESLEY ANTHONY ARNOLDI (1909-2012)
165. ix.　CLEOVA CARLITA "Girly" ARNOLDI WENCEL (1910-2004)
166. x.　WILLARD FILMORE ARNOLDI (1913-1975)

157. ORA RAYFIELD ARNOLDI Born on 25 September 1897 in Germantown, Cottonwood County, Minnesota. Ora died in Whaton, Traverse County, Minnesota on 29 July 1966. Burial at Graceville Cemetery In Graceville Township, Big Stone County, Minnesota.

158. JESSIE VIOLA ARNOLDI Born on 14 October 1898 in Milford, Brown County, Minnesota. Jessie died in Graceville, Big Stone County, Minnesota on 9 November 1994. Burial at Graceville Consolidated Cemetery in Graceville:
https://www.findagrave.com/memorial/154612225/jessie_viola_billiet

On 27 September 1919, JESSIE VIOLA ARNOLDI married CARL BILLIET, son of ANTHONY LEOPOLDUS BILLIET (1856-1936) & SERENA DOUBLER (1865-1952), in Big Stone County, Minnesota. CARL BILLIET was born in Annawan, Henry County, Illinois on 29 September 1892. He died in Graceville, Big Stone County, Minnesota on 24 December 1969.

Burial at Consolidated Graceville Cemetery in Graceville:
https://www.findagrave.com/memorial/154612104/carl_billiet

JESSIE & CARL were the parents of:
i. GORDON CARL BILLIET (1921-1999)
   WW II Veteran, Cpl in U. S. Army:
   https://www.findagrave.com/memorial/154614090/gordon_carl_billiet
ii. LELAND P. BILLIET (1922-1974)
   WW II Veteran, Staff Sgt in U. S. Army:
   https://www.findagrave.com/memorial/367117/leland_p_billiet
iii. DUANE ANTHONY "WAYNE" BILLIET (1928-2015)
   WW II Veteran, U. S. Navy, Victory Medal Recipient:
   https://www.findagrave.com/memorial/154615082/duane_anthony_billiet

> *"Duane Anthony Billiet was born December 5, 1928, in Graceville, Minnesota, to Carl and Jessie (Arnoldi) Billiet. On December 21, 1945, Wayne enlisted in the U. S. Navy and served on the USS St. Paul. He was honorably discharged October 22, 1947, receiving the World War II Victory Medal. On May 28, 1952, Wayne married Ardis "Tucky" Ellingson at the Holy Rosary Catholic Church in Graceville. He owned and operated Wayne's Body Shop in Graceville and also the Graceville Ambulance Service. Tucky passed away November 7, 2010. Wayne was a member of the Holy Rosary Catholic Church, the Jesse S. Poole American Legion Post 297, and the Graceville Fire Department. Wayne enjoyed playing cards, playing Golf with Liar's Dice and early morning socializing at Wayne's coffee shop. He also spent many hours on his wood carvings and making urns for people."*

159. ELRA LEO ARNOLDI Born on 3 October 1900 in Sleepy Eye, Brown County, Minnesota. Elra died in Wheaton, Traverse County, Minnesota on 15 October 1971. Burial at Graceville

Cemetery in Graceville Township, Big Stone County, Minnesota. WW II Veteran, Private in Army Air Forces: https://www.findagrave.com/memorial/222839329/elra_leo_arn

160. VERONICA ESTHER "VERA" ARNOLDI Born on 16 August 1902 in Sleepy Eye, Brown County, Minnesota. Veronica died in Kandiyohi County, Minnesota on 17 October 1995. Burial at Fort Snelling National Cemetery in Minneapolis, Hennepin County, Minnesota.

Sometime before 21 April 1930, VERONICA ESTHER "VERA" ARNOLDI married JUDEAN EDMUND JOHNSON, son of MARTEN JOHNSON & INGEBORG "EMMA" NAPPEN. JUDEAN JOHNSON was born 26 March 1891 in Madison, Lac Qui Parle County, Minnesota. Judean died in Minneapolis, Hennepin County, Minnesota on 11 June 1959. Burial at Fort Snelling National Cemetery in Minneapolis, Hennepin County, Minnesota, WW I Veteran, PFC CO 10 Engineers.

VERONICA & JUDEAN had no known children.

161. MAGDALENA UNA ARNOLDI Born on 12 September 1905 in Sleepy Eye, Brown County, Minnesota. Magdalena died in Roseville, Ramsey County, Minnesota on 30 April 1999. Burial at Graceville Cemetery in Graceville Township, Big Stone County, Minnesota.

162. ANGELINE KATHERINE ARNOLDI Born on 24 September 1906 in Sleepy Eye, Brown County, Minnesota. Angeline died in Albert Lea, Freeborn County, Minnesota on 2 September 1997. Burial location is unknown.

On 15 May 1928, ANGELINE KATHERINE ARNOLDI married 1. EMIL HERMAN BUDACH, son of GUSTAV ADOLPH

BUDACH SR. (1867-1947) & WILHELMINE PAULINE DAMMASCH (1866-1946), in Blue Earth, Fairbault County, Minnesota.

> NOTE: *Angeline was the 2nd wife of Emil.*

z
EMIL HERMAN BUDACH was born on 20 November 1891 in Ottawa, Lasalle County, Illinois. Emil died in Blue Earth, Fairbault County, Minnesota on 4 November 1939. Burial at Peace United Church of Christ Cemetery in Blue Earth, Minnesota: https://www.findagrave.com/memorial/23948727/emil_h_budach

ANGELINE & 1. EMIL were the parents of:
i. BETTY LOU BUDACH AVERY (1927-2014): https://www.findagrave.com/memorial/130747777/betty_lou_avery
ii. DARLEEN BUDACH ZIMMERMAN (1930-Living 10 December 2014)
iii. MARJORIE KATHERINE BUDACH BEISER (1932-Living 10 December 2014)
iv. GLADYS A BUDACH TENNIS (1934-Living 10 December 2014)
v. ALVIN JULIUS BUDACH (1936-1992)
vi. CAROL NORINE BUDACH WHEELER (1937-Living 10 December 2014)

On 24 October 1949, ANGELINE ARNOLDI married 2. FRANK ANDREW PILACZYNSKI, son of PETER PILACZYNSKI & AGNES KRAJNISK, in Albert Lea, Freeborn County, Minnesota.

> NOTE: *Angeline was the 2nd wife of Frank.*

FRANK ANDREW PILACZYNSKI was born 25 November 1889 in Fairmont Twp., Martin County, Minnesota. Frank died in Fairbault County, Minnesota on 31 July 1969. Burial at Our Lady

of Mount Carmel Cemetery in Easton, Fairbault, Minnesota:
https://www.findagrave.com/memorial/35972914/frank-a-pilaczynski

163. ELIZABETH ARNOLDI Born on 12 April 1908 in New Ulm, Brown County, Minnesota. She died in New Ulm, Brown County, Minnesota on 14 April 1908.

165. WESLEY ANTHONY ARNOLDI Born on 30 May 1909 in Sanborn, Redwood County, Minnesota. Wesley died in Pequot Lakes, Crow Wing County, Minnesota on 13 July 2012. He was 103, a Centenarian. Burial at Graceville Consolidated Cemetery in Graceville, Big Stone County, Minnesota:
https://www.findagrave.com/memorial/93648159/wesley_anthony_arnoldi

Life Legacy Personal Photo:
http://www.bainbridgefuneralhome.com/memsol.cgi?user_id=893011

> *"Funeral Mass for Wesley Anthony Arnoldi, age 103, of Pequot Lakes, Minnesota, formerly a lifelong resident of Graceville, Minnesota will be held on Thursday, July 19, 2012 at 11:00 A. M. at Holy Rosary Catholic Church in Graceville, Minnesota with Fr. Joe Vandeberg, Celebrant. Visitation will be held one hour prior to service time at the church. Interment will be in the Graceville Consolidated Cemetery. Wesley Anthony Arnoldi was born on May 30, 1909 to Peter and Mary Arnoldi in Sanborn, Minnesota. As a young boy Wesley and his family moved to the Graceville area where farming was their occupation. Wesley attended school through the eighth grade and then elected to work on the farm with his family. Wesley and Nona Kenyon were united in marriage on December 2, 1935 at the St. Barnabus Catholic Church in Barry, Minnesota. Wesley remained farming well into his late 70's when finally deciding to retire. At the age of 95, Wesley moved to Pequot Lakes to spend his remaining years with his immediate family, grandchildren and great-grandchildren. Wesley enjoyed his family and friends. He enjoyed playing cards, listening to Twins baseball games, visiting with any and all, hunting, reading western books, fishing and especially farming.*

Wesley passed away on Friday, July 13, 2012 at the Heritage House in Pequot Lakes, Minnesota. Wesley is lovingly remembered by his children: Beverly (Ordell) Buntje; Ronald Arnoldi; and Rick (Linda) Arnoldi all of Crosslake, Minnesota; grandchildren: Dana (David) Anderson; Shane (Christine) Buntje and Heather Berger; great-grandchildren: Tyler Anderson, Kendyl Anderson, Karly Anderson, Grant Buntje, Ghage Berger, Nicole Tommerdahl and Cassandra Tommerdahl and many nieces, nephews and cousins. Wesley was preceded in death by his beloved wife of fifty years Nona, an infant son Duane, his parents, three brothers: Ora, Elra and Willard, and six sisters: Jessie Billiet, Veronica Johnson, Elizabeth Arnoldi, Una Arnoldi, Angeline Pelizinski and Cleova Wencel."

On 2 December 1935, WESLEY ANTHONY ARNOLDI married NONA LAURA KENYON, daughter of CHARLES ALBERT KENYON (1868-1941) & PAULINE LENA HENNE (1879-1957), at St. Barnabus Catholic Church in Barry, Big Stone County, Minnesota. NONA KENYON was born on 23 November 1914 in Lincoln, Lancaster, Nebraska. Nona died in Graceville, Big Stone County, Minnesota on 6 May 1986. Burial at Graceville Consolidated Cemetery in Graceville:
https://www.findagrave.com/memorial/146995999/nona_laura_arnoldi

WESLEY & NONA were the parents of:
i. DUANE ARNOLDI (1938-1938)
ii. BEVERLY ANN ARNOLDI BUNTJE (1940-
iii. RONALD EUGENE ARNOLDI (1946-
iv. RICHARD JAMES (RICK) ARNOLDI (1954-

165. CLEOVA CARLITA "GIRLY" ARNOLDI Born on 28 December 1910 in Germantown, Cottonwood County, Minnesota. Cleova died in Browns Valley, Traverse County, Minnesota on 2 March 2004. Burial at Wildwood Cemetery in Wheaton, Traverse County, Minnesota:
https://www.findagrave.com/memorial/146608149/cleova_carlita_wencel

About 1932, CLEOVA ARNOLDI married FREDERICK EDWARD WENCEL, son of FRANK JOHN WENCEL (1862-1946) & THERESA ROSELLA HABERMAN (1862-1944). FREDERICK EDWARD WENCEL was born in Peever, Roberts County, South Dakota on 15 September 1904. Fred died in Wheaton, Traverse County, Minnesota on 30 July 1949. Burial at Wildwood Cemetery in Wheaton, Traverse County, Minnesota.

> *NOTE*: *Cleova Arnoldi was the 2nd wife of Fred Wencel:*
> https://www.findagrave.com/memorial/146608140/frederick_edward_wencel

CLEOVA & FRED were the parents of:
i. GLORY HELEN WENCEL SCHMITZ (1932-2018)
ii. JOY YVONNE WENCEL LEWANDOWSKI (LEONARD) (1935-Living 5 February 2018)
iii. LAMOYNE EDWARD WENCEL (1936-Living 5 February 2018)
iv. DARYL EUGENE WENCEL (1940-1945)

166. WILLARD FILMORE ARNOLDI Born on 26 February 1913 in Germantown, Cottonwood County, Minnesota. Willard died in Wheaton, Traverse County, Minnesota on 7 September 1975. Burial at Wildwood Cemetery in Wheaton, Traverse County, Minnesota. WW II Veteran, U. S. Army:
https://www.findagrave.com/memorial/146608481/willard_filmore_arnoldi

45. ROSALIA (ROSA) SCHMITT Born on 29 November 1879 in Mulligan Twp., Brown County, Minnesota. Rosa died in Homer Township, Stutsman County, North Dakota on 18 April 1957. Burial at Calvary Cemetery in Jamestown, Stutsman County,

North Dakota:
https://www.findagrave.com/memorial/123478449/rosalie-hickel

On 3 August 1903, ROSA SCHMITT married HENRY HARRISON ECKERT, son of MICHAEL ECKERT (1845-1947) & MIRANDA MERK (1852-1936), in New Ulm, Brown County, Minnesota. HENRY ECKERT was born on 25 February 1881 in New Ulm, Brown County, Minnesota. He died in Vernon, Los Angeles County, California on 2 January 1963. Burial at Rose Hills Memorial Park in Whittier, Los Angeles County, California: https://www.findagrave.com/memorial/124552131/henry-harrison-eckert

> *NOTE*: *It is unclear when Rose and Henry divorced. In the 1905 Minnesota State Census she was recorded as "Rosy Eckert", living with her parents and her brothers Nicholas, Frank, and William, in Mulligan Township. On 31 August 1916, the Williston Graphic announced that "A marriage license has been issued to Peter Hickel and Miss [Mrs] Rose Eckert, both of Ray."*

ROSA & 1. HENRY ECKERT were the parents of a son:

167. i. CHARLES ECKERT Born 2 September 1903, Died 19 September 1903 in Mulligan Twp., Brown County, Minnesota. Burial at Leavenworth, Brown County, Minnesota.

On 12 September 1916, ROSA SCHMITT ECKERT married 2. PETER PAUL HICKEL, son of ANTON JOHN HICKEL (1831-1921) & MARY ANNA ARNOLD (1841-1915), in Ray, Williams County, North Dakota. She was the 2nd wife of Peter. PETER PAUL HICKEL was born 24 June 1869 in Mankato, Blue Earth County, Minnesota. Peter died in Ray, Williams County, North Dakota on 19 July 1945. Burial at Highland Cemetery in Ray, Williams County, North Dakota:
https://www.findagrave.com/memorial/233001050/peter_hickel

ROSA & 2. PETER HICKEL were the parents of:

168. i.   VINCENT PETER HICKEL (1915-1982)
169. ii. ANITA HICKEL (1917-1932)
170. iii. INA MAE HICKEL BURES (1921-1985)

168. VINCENT PETER HICKEL Born 5 April 1915 in Brown County, Minnesota. Vincent died in Bismarck, Burleigh County, North Dakota on 5 December 1982. Burial at Highland Cemetery in Ray, Williams County, North Dakota.
https://www.findagrave.com/memorial/233002361/vincent_peter_hickel

On 13 September 1939, VINCENT PETER HICKEL married ROBINA "RUBY" FLYNN CONVEY, daughter of JOSEPH CONVEY & CATHERINE FLYNN (1889–1964) in Phillips County, Montana. ROBINA FLYNN CONVEY was born 24 February 1913 in Linlithgow, West Lothian, Scotland, United Kingdom. RUBY died in Williams County, North Dakota on 27 February 1989. Burial at Highland Cemetery in Ray, Williams County, North Dakota.
https://www.findagrave.com/memorial/233002403/robina_convey_hickel

VINCENT PETER & RUBY were the parents of:
i.   NEIL W. HICKEL (abt. 1942-)

169. ANITA HICKEL Born 29 July 1917 in North Dakota. Anita died 30 December 1932 in Williams County, North Dakota. Burial at Highland Cemetery, Hickel family plot, in Ray, Williams County, North Dakota:
https://www.findagrave.com/memorial/233001261/anita-hickel

170. INA MAE HICKEL Born 15 December 1921 in North Dakota. Ina died in Bismarck, Burleigh County, North Dakota on 25 April

1985. Burial at Bohemian Cemetery in Ross, Mountrail County, North Dakota.

In 1940, INA MAE HICKEL married LEONARD BURES, son of JOSEPH BURES (1876-1955) & EMMA SCHINDLER (1884-1972). Leonard BURES was born 25 September 1910 in Debing Township, Mountrail County, North Dakota. Leonard died in Stanley, Mountrail County, North Dakota on 30 March 1992. Burial at Bohemian Cemetery in Ross, Mountrail County, North Dakota.

INA MAE & LEONARD were the parents of:
i. LEONARD DALE BURES (1943-1955)
ii. MITCHELL BURES (1949-

46. BERTHA KATHERINE SCHMITT Born on 23 December 1880 in Mulligan Twp., Brown County, Minnesota. Bertha died in Stanley, Mountrail County, North Dakota on 7 March 1953. Burial at Fairview Cemetery in Stanley, Mountrail County, North Dakota:
https://www.findagrave.com/memorial/10207604/bertha-katherine-fitzpatrick

On 30 October 1900, BERTHA KATHERINE SCHMITT married JOSEPH JULIUS FITZPATRICK, son of MICHAEL FITZPATRICK (1853-1917) & MARY FARRELL (1859-1959), in Leavenworth, Brown, Minnesota. JOSEPH JULIUS FITZPATRICK was born on 6 August 1879 in Otisco, Waseca County, Minnesota. Joseph died in New Town, Mountrail County, North Dakota on 15 March 1957. Burial at Fairview Cemetery in Stanley, Mountrail County, North Dakota:
https://www.findagrave.com/memorial/10207605/joseph_j_fitzpatrick

BERTHA SCHMITT & JOSEPH FITZPATRICK

BERTHA & JOSEPH were the parents of
171. i. GEORGE MARSTON FITZPATRICK (1902-1968)
172. ii. JOSEPH MICHAEL FITZPATRICK (1905-1964)
173. iii. MAYNARD CHARLES FITZPATRICK (1911-1936)
174. iv. MAE KATHERINE FITZPATRICK OLSON (1915-2010)

171. GEORGE MARSTON FITZPATRICK Born 7 February 1902 in Comfrey, Brown County, Minnesota. George died in Stanley, Mountrail County, North Dakota on 13 July 1968. Burial at Fairview Cemetery in Stanley.

GEORGE MARSTON FITZPATRICK married ELLEN GUNDRUN STONE, daughter of OLAUS M. STONE (may have been STOEN) (1860-1935) & GERTRUDE KLEFSAAS (1865-1962). ELLEN GUNDRUN STONE was born on 5 July 1902 in Madison, Lac Qui Parle County, Minnesota. Ellen died in Minneapolis, Hennepin County, Minnesota on 20 June 1955. Burial at Fairview Cemetery in Stanley, Mountrail County, North Dakota.

GEORGE & ELLEN were the parents of:
i. GEORGE MARSTON FITZPATRICK Jr. (1933-2018) Korean War Veteran, U. S. Army

172. JOSEPH MICHAEL FITZPATRICK Born on 31 July 1905 in Douglas County, Minnesota. Joseph died in Stanley, Mountrail County, North Dakota on 11 September 1964. Burial at Fairview Cemetery in Stanley. WW II Veteran, Sgt., 439 Troop CARR GP U. S. Army Air Forces:
https://www.findagrave.com/memorial/10207602/joseph_m_fitzpatrick

JOSEPH MICHAEL FITZPATRICK married 1. MARGARET SULLIVAN. MARGARET SULLIVAN was born on 3 March 1909 in Minnesota. Margaret died on 27 February 1999. Burial at Saint Joseph's Catholic Cemetery in Devils Lake, Ramsey, North Dakota:
https://www.findagrave.com/memorial/122521035/margaret_fitzpatrick

JOSEPH MICHAEL FITZPATRICK & 1. MARGARET SULLIVAN were the parents of:
i. COLLEEN FITZPATRICK FOLEY (MIKE) (1927-2003): https://www.legacy.com/us/obituaries/sandiegouniontribune/name/colleen-foley-obituary?id=27713640
ii. DOROTHY J. FITZPATRICK HILL (1932- Living 6 April 2003, in Portland, Oregon)
iii. MICHAEL J. FITZPATRICK (1935-2015): https://www.findagrave.com/memorial/162868417/michael-j-fitzpatrick

JOSEPH MICHAEL FITZPATRICK married in 1945, 2. MABEL ELIZABETH TAYLOR 1908-1988:

https://www.findagrave.com/memorial/245564406/mabel_elizabeth_fitzpatrick

173. MAYNARD CHARLES FITZPATRICK Born on 9 January 1911 Idaho, Mountrail County, North Dakota. Maynard never married. He died in Valley County, Montana on 29 August 1936. Burial at Fairview Cemetery in Stanley, Mountrail County, North Dakota.

174. MAE KATHERINE FITZPATRICK Born about 1914 in Idaho Township, Mountrail County, North Dakota. Mae died in Portland, Washington County, Oregon in 2010. Burial at Finley-Sunset Hills Memorial Park in Portland, Washington County, Oregon.

On 3 February 1945, MAE KATHERINE FITZPATRICK married ARTHUR WILLIAM OLSON, son of CARL EDVARTSEN OLSON (1894-1968) & ANNA OLENA "LENA" SPJODTVOLD (1887-1980), in Sidney, Richland County, Montana. ARTHUR OLSON was born 2 March 1921 in Ross, Mountrail, North Dakota. Arthur died in Portland, Multnomah, Oregon on 3 March 2004. Burial at Finley-Sunset Hills Memorial Park in Portland, Washington County, Oregon.

MAE KATHERINE & ARTHUR had no known children.

47. CHARLES (CARL) SCHMITT Born on 8 May 1882 in Mulligan Twp., Brown County, Minnesota. Carl died in Mulligan Twp., Brown County, Minnesota on 5 January 1896. Burial at the Schmitt family plot at Japanese Martyrs Cemetery in Leavenworth, Brown County, Minnesota.

48. FRANK J. SCHMITT Born on 4 June 1883 in Mulligan Twp., Brown County, Minnesota. Frank never married. He died in Ramsey, Mower County, Minnesota on 22 October 1969. Burial at the Schmitt family plot at Japanese Martyrs Cemetery in Leavenworth, Brown County, Minnesota.

49. WILLIAM HENRY SCHMITT Born on 21 July 1887 in Mulligan Twp., Brown County, Minnesota. William never married. He died in Leavenworth, Brown County, Minnesota on 15 November 1914. Burial at the Schmitt family plot at Japanese Martyrs Cemetery in Leavenworth, Brown County, Minnesota.

WILLIAM HENRY SCHMITT

Descendants of JACOB SCHMITT & ANNA GOEDERT through their son NICHOLAS SCHMITT & MARIA MEILER:
15 Grandchildren (Bold Black)
30 Great-grandchildren (Fuchsia)
44 2x Great-grandchildren (Teal)

Chapter VI

PETER SCHMITT

6. PETER SCHMITT Born on 23 July 1848 in Johnsburg, McHenry County, Illinois. Baptism recorded on 2 August 1848 at St. Joseph Catholic Church in Wilmette, Cook County, Illinois. PETER SCHMITT (Smith) died in McHenry, McHenry County, Illinois of typhoid fever on 30 November 1883; he was 35. Buried on 2 December 1883 at St. John the Baptist Cemetery in Johnsburg, McHenry County, Illinois:
https://www.findagrave.com/memorial/68733144/peter-schmitt

Obituary in **McHenry Plaindealer, Wednesday 5 December 1883**:

> *"Peter Smith, who keeps a Saloon and Boarding House in Lansing's Block, near the depot, died on Friday last after an illness of a little over three weeks, of typhoid fever. He was a man about 34 years of age and leaves a wife and three children to mourn his loss, his funeral was held at Johnsburg on Sunday."*

> NOTE: *When Peter died in 1883 he was buried in St. John the Baptist Churchyard Cemetery in Johnsburg. His death and burial are recorded in St. John the Baptist records. It appears that Peter at some point in time possibly after the death of his wife Elizabeth in 1932, may have been reinterred at St. Mary's Catholic Cemetery in McHenry, (or his memorial stone was moved to St. Mary's Cemetery) established in 1896. Also, daughter Susanna has her memorial stone in St. Mary's Cemetery alongside that of her father and mother:*
> https://www.findagrave.com/memorial/68733173/susanna-schmitt)

Daughter Susanna died in 1876 and Peter died in 1883, but St. Mary's Cemetery was not established until 1895/96.

> *NOTE*: *The surname etched in the memorial stone of Peter is misspelled as SCHMIDT: St. Mary's Cemetery Section E Plot 2. https://www.findagrave.com/memorial/68733144/peter_schmitt*

On 22 September 1870 when PETER SCHMITT was 22, he married ELIZABETH FREUND, daughter of NICKOLAUS FREUND (1804-1891) & MARIA CATHARINA STEFFENS (1808-1877), at St. John the Baptist Catholic Church in Johnsburg, McHenry County, Illinois. ELIZABETH FREUND was born on 21 October 1849 in Luxem, Dist. Mayen, Rhineland, Prussia. Elizabeth died at the home of her son GEORGE SMITH in Woodstock, McHenry County, Illinois on 17 January 1932; she was 82. Buried on 19 January 1932 at St. Mary's Catholic Cemetery (Section E Plot 2) in McHenry, McHenry County, Illinois: https://www.findagrave.com/memorial/68733102/elizabeth_schmitt Obituary on memorial, and in McHenry Plaindealer, 21 January 1932, Front page.

St. John the Baptist Catholic Church, Johnsburg, McHenry County, Illinois
(Transcribed by MCIGS in 1985)
Early Records of St. John the Baptist Catholic Church Volume II: 1869-1882
Peter SCHMITT & Elisabeth FREUND
m 22 Sep 1870
Witnesses: Anton WEBER & Maria MÜLLER.

> *NOTE*: *Peter SCHMITT and his brother-in-law, Peter ROTHERMEL, purchased farms in 1878 in Clay County, Nebraska. Peter SCHMITT and family returned to Illinois by 1 November 1881.*

PETER & ELIZABETH were the parents of the following children. Their births and baptisms are recorded at St. John the Baptist Catholic Church in Johnsburg, McHenry County, Illinois:

50. i.   WILHELM (WILLIAM) NICOLAUS SCHMITT (1872-1924)
51. ii. CATHARINA SCHMITT WAGNER (1874-1968)
52. iii. SUSANNA SCHMITT (1876-1876)
53. iv. JOSEPH SCHMITT (1878-1878)
54. v. MARY SCHMITT (b. Dec 1879- d. bef 30 Nov. 1883)
55. vi. GEORGE STEPHEN SCHMITT (SMITH) (1882-1966)

Descendants of JACOB SCHMITT & ANNA GOEDERT:
Grandchildren (Bold Black)
Great-grandchildren (Fuchsia)
2x Great-grandchildren (Teal)

50. WILHELM NICOLAUS (WILLIAM) SCHMITT Born on the "old Schmitt homestead" on east Johnsburg-Spring Grove Road, on 28 April 1872 in Johnsburg, McHenry County, Illinois. William never married. His occupation was a carpenter and contractor, and at time of his death he was a member of the Jamestown (North Dakota) Development Company, engaged in the drilling of oil wells in Billings, Montana. William was en route to Billings when he died in an auto accident in Billings, Yellowstone County, Montana on 15 May 1924; he was 51. Burial at St. Mary's Catholic Cemetery (Section E Plot 2) in McHenry, McHenry County, Illinois:
https://www.findagrave.com/memorial/68733023/william_n_schmitt
Obituary on memorial and in McHenry Plaindealer, 29 May 1924, Front page.

51. CATHARINA (Catherine) SCHMITT Born on 28 July 1874 in Johnsburg, McHenry County, Illinois. Catharina died in Wheat Ridge, Jefferson County, Colorado in 1968; she was 94 years of age. Burial at Mount Olivet Cemetery in Wheat Ridge, Jefferson County, Colorado.
https://www.findagrave.com/memorial/130261159/catherine_wagner

On 6 September 1892 when CATHARINA SCHMITT was 18, she married JACOB C. WAGNER, son of JOHANN WAGNER (1816-1909) & CATHERINE SCHNEIDER (1825-1908), at St. John the Baptist Catholic Church in Johnsburg, McHenry County, Illinois. JACOB C. WAGNER was born on 28 January 1863 in Glenview, Cook County, Illinois. Jacob died in Denver, Denver County, Colorado on 20 March 1955; he was 92. Burial at Mount Olivet Cemetery in Wheat Ridge, Jefferson County, Colorado.
https://www.findagrave.com/memorial/130260950/jacob_c_wagner

CATHERINE & **JACOB** were parents of:
175. i. MARY ELIZABETH WAGNER FREDERICK (1893-aft 12 April 1950)
176. ii. CECILIA ELIZABETH WAGNER WILD (1896-1988)
177. iii. GEORGE JOSEPH WAGNER (1899-1987) Never Married
178. iv. WILLIAM THOMAS WAGNER (1901-1952)
179. v. VERONICA M. WAGNER LUCY (1906-1969)

175. MARY ELIZABETH WAGNER Born on 21 July 1893 in Chicago, Cook County, Illinois. Died after 12 April 1950.

On 20/21 June 1919 when MARY ELIZABETH WAGNER was 25, she married RUDOLPH ARNOLD FREDERICK, son of THEODORE FREDERICK & NATHALIE BRADEN in St. Joseph County, Indiana. RUDOLPH FREDERICK was born on 23 April 1885 in Hanover, Prussia (Germany). Rudolph died in Denver County, Colorado in November 1970; he was 85.

MARY & RUDOLPH were the parents of:
i.   ARNOLD C. FREDERICK (1921-1981)
ii. DORIS MAE FREDERICK HLADEK (1924-1998)
iii. EDWIN F. FREDERICK (1926-)

176. CECILIA ELIZABETH WAGNER Born 7 August 1896 in Evanston, Cook County, Illinois. Cecilia died in Wheat Ridge, Jefferson County, Colorado on 11 September 1988; she was 92. Burial at Mount Olivet Cemetery in Wheat Ridge:
https://www. findagrave. com/memorial/131361174/cecilia_elizabeth_wild

On 2 September 1918 when CECILIA ELIZABETH WAGNER was 22, she married JOHN LOUIS WILD, son of JOHN WILD & ELIZABETH YONKER, in Denver, Denver County, Colorado. JOHN LOUIS WILD was born on 27 November 1895 in Rochester, Monroe County, New York. John died in Denver County, Colorado on 1 November 1958; he was 62. Burial at Mount Olivet Cemetery in Wheat Ridge, Jefferson County, Colorado:
https://www. findagrave. com/memorial/131361068/john_louis_wild

CECILIA & JOHN had no children recorded in 1920-1930 Census records.

177. GEORGE JOSEPH WAGNER Born on 31 May 1899 in Chicago, Cook County, Illinois. George died in Wheat Ridge,

Jefferson County, Colorado on 3 May 1987; he was 87. Burial at Mount Olivet Cemetery in Wheat Ridge.
https://www.findagrave.com/memorial/130258340/george-joseph-wagner

On 15 February 1922, GEORGE JOSEPH WAGNER married AGNES LEIDGEN, daughter of HERMAN LEIDGEN (1863-1906) and HELENA "LENA" LUND or LUNT (1870-1936), in Denver, Jefferson County, Colorado. AGNES LEIDGEN was born about 1901. Agnes remarried to JAMES PAPPAS (1888-1975) on 4 January 1935 in Cache County, Utah. Per the 1950 Census, Agnes was a teletype operator. Agnes died in 1994 in Ogden, Weber County, Utah. Burial at Lindquists Memorial Gardens of the Wasatch in South Ogden, Weber County, Utah.
https://www.findagrave.com/memorial/169672664/agnes-pappas

GEORGE & AGNES had no known children.

178. WILLIAM THOMAS WAGNER Born on 26 April 1901 in Evanston, Cook County, Illinois. William died in Wheat Ridge, Jefferson County, Colorado on 25 December 1952; he was 51. Burial at Mount Olivet Cemetery in Wheat Ridge:
https://www. findagrave. com/memorial/130208137/william-thomas-wagner

On 26 July 1923 when WILLIAM THOMAS WAGNER was 22, he married MINNIE MAE HANLON, daughter of HARRY HOLMES HANLON (1872-1952) & KATHERINE E. KIRSHER (1881-1966), in Denver, Denver County, Colorado. MINNIE MAE HANLON was born on 18 April 1905 in Pocatello, Bannock County, Idaho. Minnie died in Denver, Denver County, Colorado on 11 November 2002; she was 97. Burial at Mount Olivet Cemetery in Wheat Ridge, Jefferson County, Colorado:

https://www.findagrave.com/memorial/130208176/minnie_mae_wagner

WILLIAM & MINNIE were the parents of:
i. DOROTHY M. WAGNER SCHEIER (1924-
ii. WILLIAM JOSEPH WAGNER (1926-2015)
   WW II Veteran, S1 U.S. Navy

179. VERONICA M. WAGNER Born on 17 May 1906 in Denver City, Denver County, Colorado. Veronica died in Denver City, Denver County, Colorado in June 1969; she was 63. Burial at Mount Olivet Catholic Cemetery in Wheat Ridge, Jefferson County, Colorado:
https://www.findagrave.com/memorial/187151794/veronica-m-lucy

On 29 November 1928, when VERONICA M. WAGNER was 22, she married ROBERT DANIEL LUCY, son of Dr. DANIEL LUCY (1860-1941) & MARGARET LEWIS (1879-1953), in Denver, Denver County, Colorado. ROBERT D. LUCY was born on 22 February 1905 in Denver City, Denver County, Colorado. Robert died in Denver City, Denver County, Colorado on 11 June 1996; he was 91. Burial at Mount Olivet Cemetery in Wheat Ridge, Jefferson County, Colorado:
https://www.findagrave.com/memorial/125733892/robert_daniel_lucy

NOTE: *Robert Lucy married 2. GLADYS CATHERINE HILL.*

VERONICA & ROBERT were the parents of:
i. DANIEL RICHARD LUCY (1930-
ii. PATRICIA LUCY (1933-
iii. VERONICA LUCY (1936-

52. SUSANNA SCHMITT Born on 18 September 1876 in Johnsburg, McHenry County, Illinois. Susanna died on 23 September 1876. She was buried at St. John the Baptist Cemetery in Johnsburg.

> *NOTE*: *It appears that at some point in time, Susanna, like her father Peter, was later reinterred at St. Mary's Catholic Cemetery in McHenry, established in 1895/96.*

Susanna's birth, baptism, death and burial were recorded at St. John the Baptist Catholic Church in Johnsburg. Susanna's memorial stone from 1876, is in the same plot as her mother, Elizabeth SCHMITT who died in 1932. Susanna's memorial stone from 1876 (surname etched in stone is SCHMIDT) is located in Section E Plot 2 at St. Mary's Catholic Cemetery:
https://www.findagrave.com/memorial/68733173/susanna-schmitt

St. John the Baptist Catholic Church, Johnsburg, McHenry County, Illinois:
(Transcribed by MCIGS in 1985)
Early Records 1869-1882 Volume II
Page 21
Susanna SCHMITT
b 18 Sep 1876 bap 18 Sep 1876
d/o Peter SCHMITT & Elisabeth FREUND
Wit: Mathias MAI [MAY] & Susanna MILLER
Page 53
Susanna SCHMIDT d 23 Sep 1876 bur 24 Sep 1876.

53. JOSEPH SCHMITT Born on 17 July 1878 in Johnsburg, McHenry County, Illinois. Joseph died on 19 July 1878. Burial at St. John the Baptist Cemetery in Johnsburg. Burial location is unknown per cemetery office.

54. GEORGE STEPHEN SCHMITT (SMITH) Born on 9 April 1882 in Johnsburg, McHenry County, Illinois. At some point in time George changed the spelling of his surname to SMITH. George died in McHenry, McHenry County, Illinois on 2 March 1966; he was 83. Buried on 5 March 1966 at Woodstock Memorial Park in Woodstock, McHenry County, Illinois.

> *NOTE*: There is no memorial stone at the grave site of GEORGE SMITH.
> https://www.findagrave.com/memorial/148820723/george_stephen_smith

On 1 October 1907 when GEORGE SCHMITT was 25, he married ANNA JOSEPHINA (JOSEPHINE ANN) ENGELN, daughter of MATHIAS ENGELN (1844-1910) & BARBARA SCHREINER (1853-1950) in McHenry County, Illinois. ANNA JOSEPHINA ENGELN was born on 19 November 1882 in Johnsburg, McHenry County, Illinois. Josephine died in Woodstock, McHenry County, Illinois on 6 March 1956; she was 73. Burial at St. Mary's Catholic Cemetery in McHenry, McHenry County, Illinois:
https://www.findagrave.com/memorial/68733060/josephine_ann_smith

GEORGE & JOSEPHINE ANN were the parents of a son:
180. GEORGE WILLIAM SMITH Born on 18 April 1910 in Kenosha, Kenosha County, Wisconsin. George William Smith died in Woodstock, McHenry County, Illinois on 20 February 1958; he was 47. Burial at Woodstock Memorial Park in Woodstock:
https://www.findagrave.com/memorial/120205765/george_w_smith

> *NOTE*: Between 1930 and 1940 census, GEORGE WILLIAM SMITH was married, then later divorced with no known children. Source: 1940 census, George is recorded as 'Divorced.'

Descendants of JACOB SCHMITT & ANNA GOEDERT through their son PETER SCHMITT & ELIZABETH FREUND:
6 grandchildren (Bold Black)
6 great-grandchildren (Fuchsia)
8 2x great-grandchildren (Teal)

INDEX

INDEX

A
Adams, Albert Vernie 59
Adams, Alzina Mae 59
Adams, Elizabeth 57
Adams, Frieda Rosa 59
Adams, Irma Viola 59
Adams, John 57
Adolphi, Anna Maria 35
Agusta, Justina 26
Albright, Mae 59
Althoff, Elizabeth Gertrude 102
Amundson, Edna 136
Anderson, Albert Franklin 95
Anderson, Calvin Raymond 95
Anderson, Elisabeth Jane 95
Anderson, Eugene Albert 95
Anderson, Frederick John 95
Anderson, Karly 143
Anderson, Kendyl 143
Anderson, Signa Marie 52
Anderson, Zara 95
Arnold, Mary Anna 145
Arnoldi, Angeline Katherine 138
Arnoldi, Beverly Ann 143
Arnoldi, Duane 143
Arnoldi, Elizabeth 138
Arnoldi, Elra Leo 138
Arnoldi, Jessie Viola 138
Arnoldi, Magdalena Una 138
Arnoldi, Michael 133
Arnoldi, Ora Rayfield 138
Arnoldi, Peter Mathew 137
Arnoldi, Richard James 143
Arnoldi, Ronald Eugene 143
Arnoldi, Veronica M 138
Arnoldi, Wesley Henry 138
Arnoldi, Willard B 138

B
Barker, Mary Permelia 124
Bartlett, Sarah 123
Beach, Annie Mae 83
Behm, Adam 45
Behm, Anthony J 46
Behm, Evelyn S 46
Behm, Florence Margaret 47
Behm, Frances Ann 47
Behm, George Marcus 45
Behm, Helen Mary 47
Behm, Isidor Michael 45
Behm, James Isador 47
Behm, Lucille Mary 46
Behm, Marcus Adam 47
Behm, Martin Albert 46
Behm, Mary Ann 47
Behm, Ralph W 47
Behm, Raymond J 47
Behm, Robert Joseph 46
Behm, Rose 47
Behm, Viola 47
Behm, Virginia 47
Beiser, Marjorie 137
Bell, Barbara Mary 26
Berger, Ghage 143
Berger, Heather 143
Bethold, Adele 109
Billiet, Anthony Leopoldus 138
Billiet, Carl 138
Billiet, Duane Anthony 139
Billiet, Gordon Carl 139
Billiet, Jessie 143
Billiet, Leland P 139
Blackburn, Catherine 88
Blake, Bertha Katherine 27
Blake, Edwin H 27
Blake, Ernest 27
Blake, G. Frank 27
Blake, Helen 68
Blake, Joseph 27
Blake, Leona 27
Blake, Olive Helen 27
Blake, Phillip 26
Bohr, Ernest Michael 100
Bohr, Genevive Julia 100
Bohr, George 100
Bohr, Michael 99
Bohr, Nicholas 99
Boley, Charles John 94
Boley, Christopher Gottlieb 94
Boley, Gottlieb Frederick 94
Boley, Kenneth Nicholas 94
Bonnemier, Mary 84
Braden, Theodore 157
Brennecke, Edward 56 (1933)
Brennecke, Eugene William 55
Brennecke, Evelyn Irene 55
Brennecke, George Edward 56 (1933)
Brennecke, George Ferdinand 55
Brennecke, Kathryn Gertrude 55
Brennecke, Mildred Susan 55
Broughton, George Mcclellan 88
Broughton, Gertrude 89
Buch, Joseph 99
Buch, Magdalena 99
Budach Sr., Gustav 140
Budach, Alvin Julius 141
Budach, Betty Lou 141
Budach, Carol Norine 141
Budach, Darleen 141
Budach, Emil Herman 140
Budach, Gladys A 141
Budach, Marjorie Katherine 141
Bumgarner, Constance 83
Bumgarner, John Bryan 83
Bunger, Henry 125
Bunger, William Joseph 125
Bures, Joseph 147
Bures, Leonard 147
Bures, Leonard Dale 147
Bures, Mitchell 147

C-D
Carolus (Fr.), 79
Chamberlin, Louise 110
Chamberlin, Rollo Guy 110
Craig, Rachel 24
Dammasch, Wilhelmine Filmore 141
Dancy, Irma Arvilla 132
Densmore, Fannie Josephine 110
Doubler, Serena 138
Drach, Louise Mary 47
Dutzler, Albert John 37
Dutzler, Cecilia 37
Dutzler, Clara Susanne 37
Dutzler, John Joseph 37
Dutzler, Joseph Edward 37
Dutzler, Julia 37
Dutzler, Leonard Henry 37
Dutzler, Michael 37
Dutzler, Vitus Leon 37

E
Eckert, Charles 145
Eckert, Henry 145
Eckert, Michael 145
Eirich, Richard Henry 127
Eirich, Robert Luther 126
Engeln, Anna Josephina 161
Engeln, Mathias 161
Erlandson, Clara Myrtle 116
Erlandson, John 115

Blue=Grandchildren; Red=Great-grandchildren; Green=2x Great-grandchildren

INDEX

F
Farrell, Mary 147
Felper, Dorothy Mae 60
Felper, Harry Lloyd 60
Felper, Jean Ann 60
Felper, Leland Anthony 59
Felper, Norbert Leland 60
Felper, Susan Nina 60
Felper, Thomas 59
Firnbach, Margaretha 38
Fitzpatrick Jr., George Marston 149
Fitzpatrick, Colleen 149
Fitzpatrick, Dorothy 149
Fitzpatrick, George Marston 148
Fitzpatrick, Joseph Julius 147
Fitzpatrick, Joseph Michael 148
Fitzpatrick, Mae Katherine 148
Fitzpatrick, Maynard Charles 148
Fitzpatrick, Michael J 149
Flint, Irving Lester 101
Flint, Robert Ellis 101
Flint, Roel Irene 101
Flynn, Catherine 146
Flynn, Robina 146
Fowler, Charles Arthur 63
Franke, Theresa 56
Frederick, Arnold C 157
Frederick, Doris Mae 157
Frederick, Edwin F 157
Frederick, Rudolph 157
Frett, Catharina 113
Frett, Nicolaus 11
Freund, Bernice Elizabeth 106
Freund, Caroline 43
Freund, Christine Marie 104
Freund, Elizabeth 154
Freund, Evelyn Louise 114
Freund, Frank Joseph 114
Freund, Helena 97
Freund, Johann Peter 74
Freund, Michael 97
Freund, Nickolaus 154
Freund, Orville 106
Freund, Peter 74
Freund, Peter Martin 103
Freund, Susanna 74
Freund, Susanna Rosa 98

G
Gibbs, Russell William 110
Ginder, Richard 72
Goedert-Schmitt, Susanna 14
Goedert, Anna Gertrud 13 (1806)
Goedert, Wilhelm 13
Goergen, Agnes 70
Goergen, Joseph 70
Goergen, Mathias 24
Goldstein, Gertrude 101
Green, Sarah 127
Guino, Louise 86
Guino, Walter B 86

H
Halfmann, Margaretha 74
Halsey, Hannah Martha 53
Hand, Henrietta 52
Hanlon, Harry Holmes 158
Hanlon, Minnie Mae 158
Harper, Laura Ann 131
Haskin, Granville 131
Haskin, Rosa 132
Hayes, Linda 133
Hayes, Noreen 133
Hayes, Stephen Alzina 132
Hayes, Thomas Marie 132
Heimer, Arthur John 69
Heimer, Irene Josephine 69
Heimer, Laverne Paul 69
Heimer, Leon Jerome 69
Heimer, Ralph Arthur 69
Heimer, Wilmer Peter 69
Hemling, Adelheid 61
Hennessy, Nellie 81
Herbes, Lucy 42
Hertel, Maria 45
Hertzfeldt, Charles 134
Hess, Nicholas 74
Hess, Susanna 74
Hickel, Anita 146
Hickel, Anton John 145
Hickel, Ina Mae 146
Hickel, Neil W 146
Hickel, Peter Paul 145
Hickel, Vincent Sarah 146
Hill, Gladys Catherine 159
Hiller, Susanna 97
Hingst, Louise 82
Hoemann, Johann 79
Huemann, Clara 68
Huemann, Mathias 22
Huemann, Nicholas 68
Humann, Anna 22

J
Johnson, Judean 140
Johnson, Marten 140
Johnson, Petrie 88
Justen, Anna Maria 113
Justen, Elizabeth 115
Justen, Elizabeth Agnes 113
Justen, Eugene James 114
Justen, Ferdinand Jacob 113
Justen, Friedrich 113 (1905)
Justen, Friedrich Bernard 113 (1906)
Justen, Gerald William 114
Justen, Johann R 113
Justen, John J 114 (1932)
Justen, John Joseph 112 (1844)
Justen, Joseph 113
Justen, Susanna 113
Justen, Susanna Katherine 114
Justen, William Henry 113

K
Kaehler, Carl 124
Kaehler, Wilhelmina Pauline 124
Keil, Caroline Marie 43
Keil, Hubert 43
Kennebeck, Anna Margaretha 102
Kennebeck, Anna Maria 92
Kennebeck, Arthur Floyd 99
Kennebeck, Arthur Nicolaus 103
Kennebeck, Bernard Joseph 92
Kennebeck, Bernard Nicholas 99
Kennebeck, Bernard Vernon 107
Kennebeck, Ceceilia 92
Kennebeck, Cecelia 99
Kennebeck, Clara Cathryn 93
Kennebeck, Daniel Jacob 98
Kennebeck, David Joseph 107
Kennebeck, Donald J 98
Kennebeck, Donald Raymond 98
Kennebeck, Doris Jean 98
Kennebeck, Earl John 104
Kennebeck, Edna Rose 98
Kennebeck, Edward Joseph 103
Kennebeck, Elisabeth 92 (1890)
Kennebeck, Elisabeth 103 (1898)

Blue=Grandchildren; Red=Great-grandchildren; Green=2x Great-grandchildren

INDEX

Kennebeck, Elizabeth Louise 104
Kennebeck, Elizabeth Pauline 94
Kennebeck, Elmer George 93
Kennebeck, Elvera Mary 107
Kennebeck, Emma Schaefer 99
Kennebeck, Gayle 110
Kennebeck, Genevieve Elizabeth 61
Kennebeck, Geraldine Anne 98
Kennebeck, Harold J 93
Kennebeck, Heinrich 92 (1887)
Kennebeck, Heinrich 103 (1895)
Kennebeck, Heinrich Joseph 92 (1893)
Kennebeck, Henry Joseph 103 (1896)
Kennebeck, James Allen 98
Kennebeck, Jeanette 99
Kennebeck, John 103
Kennebeck, John Henry 61
Kennebeck, Joseph 103 (1895)
Kennebeck, Joseph 103 (1901)
Kennebeck, Katherine 96
Kennebeck, Katherine Anna 92
Kennebeck, Linda 110
Kennebeck, Lorraine 99
Kennebeck, Marcella 103
Kennebeck, Marie 104
Kennebeck, Nicholas 92
Kennebeck, Nicolaus Bernard 103
Kennebeck, Pauline 64
Kennebeck, Pauline Josephine 61
Kennebeck, Raymond Henry 99
Kennebeck, Richard 98
Kennebeck, Teresa 103
Kennebeck, Theodore 103
Kennebeck, William John 61
Kerling, Katharina 115
Kernebeck, Johann Bernard 61
Kimball, Hannah 136
Kirby, Maurice William 85
Kirsher, Katherine 158
Klapperich, Anna Maria 26
Klapperich, Arthur Anton 26
Klapperich, (Sr.) Barbara 28
Klapperich, Barbara Ann 28
Klapperich, Edward 26
Klapperich, Herman Joseph 28
Klapperich, Isabella Helen 28
Klapperich, Martha Maria 26
Klapperich, Mathias 26
Klapperich, Michael 26
Klapperich, Nicholas 28

Klapperich, Robert John 28
Klapperich, Stephan Elwyn 27
Klapperich, Susanna 112
Klassen, Marie Catherine 92
Klefsaas, Gertrude 148
Klein, Anna 18
Knoeppels, Margaretha 74
Kvislen, Adolph 136
Kvislen, Margaret 136

L
Lah, Bernadine 125
Laws, Martha Susan 83
Leidgen, Agnes 158
Leidgen, Herman 158
Lent, Addison 123
Lent, Henry 124
Lent, Henry Edward 123
Lent, Leland Charles 124
Lent, Lottie Lillian 123
Lenzen, Albert Bernard 39
Lenzen, Anna Cecelia 36
Lenzen, Antoinette 42
Lenzen, Bernard Albert 36
Lenzen, Bernard J 44
Lenzen, Catherine 44
Lenzen, Cecilia Catherine 44
Lenzen, Clara E 44
Lenzen, Clarence I 45
Lenzen, Edward Michael 39
Lenzen, Eugene Vianney 42
Lenzen, Florence Mary 45
Lenzen, Frances H. 43
Lenzen, Frederick Richard 39
Lenzen, Herman Joseph 42
Lenzen, Jerome William 42
Lenzen, Johann 21
Lenzen, Johann Joseph 36
Lenzen, John B 45
Lenzen, John Joseph 38
Lenzen, Joseph Frank 36
Lenzen, Joseph William 45
Lenzen, Josephine Catherine 44
Lenzen, Leo John 39
Lenzen, Leonard Henry 36
Lenzen, Loretta Mary 44
Lenzen, Marcella 39
Lenzen, Margaretha Eva 36
Lenzen, Maria B. 36
Lenzen, Maria Catherina 46

Lenzen, Maria M. 36
Lenzen, Martin Anthony 39
Lenzen, Mary Agnes 44
Lenzen, Michael 48
Lenzen, Michael George 36
Lenzen, Michael John 35
Lenzen, Phyliss 42
Lenzen, Roman John 42
Lenzen, Rose Gertrude 44
Lenzen, Susanna Margaret 36
Lenzen, Theresa 39
Lenzen, William George 36
Lewis, Margaret 159
Loecher, Mathias 67
Loecher, Mathilda 67
Lovell, Parmelia 63
Lucy, Daniel Richard 159
Lucy, Patricia 159
Lucy, Robert 159
Lucy, Veronica Peter 159
Lund, Helena 158

M
Mai, Mathias 160
Marangi, Carmela 108
Mathias, Vernon Esther 68
Matthews, Mary Alice 84
Matthews, Stephen Elwyn 83 (1859)
Matthews, William Valentine 83 (1891)
Matthews, William Stephen 84 (1927)
Mauer, Angela 72
Mauer, Frank 71
Mayer, Allan Arthur 69
Mayer, Anthony 72
Mayer, Arlene Isabella 68
Mayer, Clarence 69
Mayer, Darrell Frederick 69
Mayer, Deelynn 72
Mayer, Edward William 66
Mayer, Elmer Joseph 68
Mayer, Ernest Peter 66
Mayer, Eugene Joseph 67
Mayer, Glen Alois 68
Mayer, Herbert L 66
Mayer, Herbert Leonard 70
Mayer, James Edward 67
Mayer, Janice Marion 70
Mayer, Johann 66
Mayer, John H 70
Mayer, Joseph Robert 66

Blue=Grandchildren; Red=Great-grandchildren; Green=2x Great-grandchildren

INDEX

Mayer, Joyce 72
Mayer, Leona 66
Mayer, Madonna Martha 70
Mayer, Marcella Anna 66
Mayer, Maria Anna 103
Mayer, Martha Mary 66
Mayer, Michael M 66
Mayer, Ralph 66
Mayer, Raymond Nicholas 66
Mayer, Romanus Herbert 68
Mayer, Shirley L 70
Mayer, Thomas 72
Mayer, Vernon 68
McCarty, Mary Ann 49
McDaniel, Jack Nolton 52
McDaniel, Reuben Broughton 52
Meiler, Anton 120
Meiler, Maria 120
Merk, Miranda 145
Michels, Ethel Catherine 34
Michels, Hazel Leona 35
Michels, Jack Nicholas 35
Michels, Joseph Florian 33
Michels, Joseph Leon 34
Michels, Patricia 34
Michels, Peter 33
Michels, Ruth Marie 34
Michels, Wilmer Kathryn 34
Middendorf, Catherine 101
Middendorf, Henry 101
Miller, Agnes Irene 57
Miller, Allen Ralph 58
Miller, Allvina 109
Miller, Anne Mae 50
Miller, Anthony Jacob 115
Miller, Arthur A 50
Miller, Benjamin Clifford 57
Miller, Benjamin Rolfe 54
Miller, Bernard J 48
Miller, Darlene 58
Miller, Douglas 51
Miller, Emma Grace 54
Miller, Estelle M 115
Miller, Eunice R 56
Miller, Eva 42
Miller, Floyd Hubert 56
Miller, Frank 115
Miller, Harvey John 54
Miller, Jacob 109
Miller, Joan 58

Miller, Johann William 51
Miller, John William 48
Miller, Joseph 58
Miller, Joseph Henry 54
Miller, Josephine Miller 57
Miller, Katharine 48
Miller, Kenneth John 56
Miller, Lauren Raymond 58
Miller, Lucille Alzina 54
Miller, Margaret Theresa 57
Miller, Maria 48
Miller, Marion Ellen 56
Miller, Martha Blanche 54
Miller, Martin Louis 57
Miller, Mathias 42
Miller, Michael Nicolas 48
Miller, Pauline Joyce 58
Miller, Penelope 51
Miller, Peter William 57
Miller, Ralph 58
Miller, Raymond 57
Miller, Richard John 115
Miller, Rita Catherine 56
Miller, Sarah S 115
Miller, Susanna 48
Miller, Wilhelm Nicolaus 52
Miller, William Henry 54
Miller, William James 48
Mohr, Maria Gertrud 13
Mongeau, Isabelle 108
Mueller, Agnes Elizabeth 25
Mueller, Anita Leona 30
Mueller, Anna 20
Mueller, Anna 23
Mueller, Anna Maria 20
Mueller, Arnold Mathias 25
Mueller, Carl 25
Mueller, Christina 23 (1889)
Mueller, Christina 23 (1891)
Mueller, Cyrilla Elizabeth 29
Mueller, Delphin Carl 30
Mueller, Elizabeth 20
Mueller, Elizabeth 24
Mueller, Elmer Joseph 30
Mueller, Emil Frederich 30
Mueller, Emma 91
Mueller, Esther Marie 25
Mueller, Evelyn Helen 30
Mueller, Francis Xavier 25
Mueller, Gertrud 20

Mueller, Helena 24
Mueller, Irene Viola 30
Mueller, Johann 91
Mueller, Johann Wilhelm 20
Mueller, John 30
Mueller, John Joseph 23
Mueller, Josephina 20
Mueller, Josephine 23
Mueller, Lavern Stephen 30
Mueller, Lizzie 21
Mueller, Magdalena 20
Mueller, Margaretha 23
Mueller, Maria "Mary" 20
Mueller, Maria K. 20
Mueller, Maria Katharina 35
Mueller, Maria M. 20
Mueller, Martha 25
Mueller, Marvin Joseph 30
Mueller, Mary 23
Mueller, Mary Ann 30
Mueller, Maxine 30
Mueller, Nicholas 23
Mueller, Nicolaus 20
Mueller, Nikolaus 20
Mueller, Paul Joseph 25
Mueller, Peter 20
Mueller, Peter Henry 20
Mueller, Raymond 25
Mueller, Reynold Joseph 25
Mueller, Rosina 25
Mueller, Susanna 20
Mueller, Viola V. 30
Mueller, Wilhelm 20
Mueller, William Joseph 25
Müller, Emma 61
Müller, Johann 18
Müller, Maria 154
Müller, Nikolaus 18
Müller, William 23
Murphy, Mary 136
Murphy, Monica 136
Murphy, Theresa Kasper 136
Murphy, William Stephen 135
Musser, Carolina 38

N

Nappen, Ingeborg 140
Nichol, Elizabeth Barbara 127
Nicholas, John 35
Nimsgern Sr., William Bernard 64

Blue=Grandchildren; Red=Great-grandchildren; Green=2x Great-grandchildren

INDEX

Nimsgern, Frank 63
Nimsgern, Joan Mary 64
Nimsgern, Joseph Matthew 64
Nimsgern, Louis 64
Nimsgern, Rosa Catherine 107
NN, Elinor 130
NN, Gladys 51

O
O'Brien, Lois 130
O'Dell, Isaac Lacey 128
O'Dell, Katherine Mary 128
Olson, Arthur William 150
Olson, Carl Edvartsen 150
Opal, Mary Grace 90

P-Q
Pace, Ernest 53
Pace, Esther 53
Pace, Florence 53
Pace, Louis 53
Padden, Agnes 66
Pappas, James 158
Pelizinski, Angeline 143
Penney, Susan Mable 53
Perkinson, Marilyn 90
Perkinson, William John 90
Petersen, Christian 88
Petersen, John Christian 88
Peterson, Christina Margaret 95
Phelps, Elizabeth 128
Pilaczynski, Frank Andrew 141
Pritchett, Adele 109
Pulvermacher, Catharina Maria 78
Pytlikova, Josephina Anna 94
Quinn, Ellen 85

R
Renz, Barbara Ann 55
Renz, Catherine 56
Richardson, Lucinda 126
Riddle, Clara 58
Ritter, Nina Maude 59
Roberts, Elias Jasper 130
Roberts, Susan Nina 130
Robinson, Edwin 27
Rosing, Maria Gertrude 43
Rossdeutcher, Clara Cecilia 47
Rossdeutcher, Karl 47
Rothermel, Peter 154

Rowe, Delbert Lester 124
Rowe, Elizabeth J 125
Rowe, Russell Delbert 125
Rowe, Warren Anthony 125
Rowe, William Howard 124

S
Sabel, Christian 86
Sabel, Elizabeth 87
Sauther, Maria Anna 66
Schaefer, Amy 90
Schaefer, Anna 80 (1862)
Schaefer, Anna 80 (1874)
Schaefer, Anna Maria 80
Schaefer, Annie 102
Schaefer, Benno Joseph 32
Schaefer, Catharina Pauline 100
Schaefer, Catherine 63
Schaefer, Conrad 33
Schaefer, Donald Henry 89
Schaefer, Earl Gordon 89
Schaefer, Eleanore Lillian 113
Schaefer, Eleanore Mae 101
Schaefer, Elisabeth 80
Schaefer, Elizabeth Margaret 33
Schaefer, Elmer John 113
Schaefer, Emma 91
Schaefer, Florence Emeline 32
Schaefer, Frederick William 32
Schaefer, Gertrude 87
Schaefer, Henry J 87
Schaefer, Herbert Alphonse 32
Schaefer, Jacob 80
Schaefer, James G 101
Schaefer, Johann 78
Schaefer, John A 80
Schaefer, John W 100
Schaefer, Joseph 31
Schaefer, Joseph Albert 113
Schaefer, Magdalena 87
Schaefer, Marcella Elizabeth 32
Schaefer, Mary 87
Schaefer, Mathias 31
Schaefer, Mathias 80
Schaefer, Megan 90
Schaefer, Melissa 90
Schaefer, Michael 80
Schaefer, Mickey 90
Schaefer, Nicolaus 80
Schaefer, Nicolaus Peter 80

Schaefer, Nikolaus 78
Schaefer, Norbert Ernest 32
Schaefer, Paul Mathias 32
Schaefer, Peter 113
Schaefer, Rita 32
Schaefer, Robert 89
Schaefer, Roger 33
Schaefer, Vernon Mathias 32
Schaefer, Wilbert Bernard 101
Schaeffer Sr., Donald 89
Schaeffer, Alice Elizabeth 81
Schaeffer, Barbara 86
Schaeffer, Catherine 86
Schaeffer, Catherine Gertrude 81
Schaeffer, Frederick George 81
Schaeffer, George N.G. 80
Schaeffer, Henry John 81
Schaeffer, Jack F 86
Schaeffer, Jeanette 86
Schaeffer, Milton J 81
Schaeffer, Susanna Rosa 81
Scheid, George 92
Scheid, Laura Kathryn 92
Schiller, Pauline 124
Schindler, Emma 147
Schmidt, Elisabeth 101
Schmidt, Susanna 160
Schmitt, Anna Catharina 99
Schmitt, Anna Maria 14
Schmitt, Anton 121
Schmitt, Bertha Katherine 122
Schmitt, Catharina 155
Schmitt, Charles 122
Schmitt, Elizabeth 121
Schmitt, Elsie Vernia 134
Schmitt, Emery Nicholas 134
Schmitt, Evata Marie 134
Schmitt, Frank J 122
Schmitt, George Stephen 155
Schmitt, Gertrud 14
Schmitt, Gertrude 121
Schmitt, Helena 121
Schmitt, Jeffery 137
Schmitt, John G 121
Schmitt, Joseph 121 (1874)
Schmitt, Joseph 155 (1878)
Schmitt, Joseph M 136
Schmitt, Joy 137
Schmitt, Julie Ann 136
Schmitt, Kate 127
Schmitt, Katherine 121

Blue=Grandchildren; Red=Great-grandchildren; Green=2x Great-grandchildren

I N D E X

Schmitt, Lowell Meiler 134
Schmitt, Margaret Ann 132
Schmitt, Margaretha 33
Schmitt, Maria 120
Schmitt, Mary 155
Schmitt, Mary K 122
Schmitt, Mary Katherine 13
Schmitt, Mathias Peter 121
Schmitt, Michael 14
Schmitt, Nicholas 14
Schmitt, Nicolaus Joseph 121
Schmitt, Peter 14
Schmitt, Rosa 145
Schmitt, Rosalia 122
Schmitt, Susanna 155
Schmitt, Susanna 91
Schmitt, Verna Joseph 134
Schmitt, Wilhelm 155
Schmitt, William Henry 122
Schneider, Catherine 156
Schneider, Christina 22
Schnorr, Catharina 99
Schreiner, Barbara 161
Schumacher, Dora 98
Schwartz, William 108
Scott, Hazell Jane 126
Scott, Henry Charles 126
Sewell, Eleanor 84
Sewell, Harry George 84
Sewell, Joseph M 85
Sewell, Kathleen 85
Sewell, Rita 85
Seymour-Miller, Joseph John 49
Seymour, Burge Miles 49
Seymour, Mary 49
Seymour, Miles Newcomb 49
Seymour, William J 49
Shaeffer, Mary Agnes 81
Shue, Elizabeth Sophia 96
Smith, Elizabeth 69
Smith, George Stephen 161
Smith, George William 161
Smith, Justina Augusta 23
Smith, Mary 50
Sonnek, Andrew 129
Sonnek, Christine 129
Spjodtvold, Anna Olena 150
Spoerl, Anna Margaret 39
Steffens, Maria Catharina 154
Steiger, Sarah Mary 28
Stilling, Henry 102

Stocks, Frieda 54
Stoffel, Elizabeth Margaret 44
Stoffel, Joseph 43
Stone, Ellen Gundrun 148
Stone, Olaus 148
Strang, Anna 90
Sullivan, Margaret 149
Swanson, Charles Arthur 124

T
Taylor, Mabel Elizabeth 149
Tekampe, Andrew Isidore 38
Tekampe, Christina Margaret 41
Tekampe, John Michael 38
Tekampe, Joseph 40
Tekampe, Joseph Vitus 41
Tekampe, Laura Margaret 38
Tekampe, Leo John 41
Tekampe, Ludwina 38
Tekampe, Margaret Mary 41
Tekampe, Martha Catherine 41
Tekampe, Oscar 38
Tekampe, Ralph Michael 38
Tekampe, Regina Catherine 40
Tekampe, Rosina Anna 38
Tekampe, William 37
Thelen, Catharina 109
Theurer, Auguste Mathilde 135
Thome, Elizabeth 29
Thome, John 28
Tonyan, Henry 102
Tordoff, Jessie 62
Torrey, Clifford Paul 129
Torrey, Eleanor A 130
Torrey, Ervin Dewitt 128
Torrey, Gene Irving 130
Torrey, John Alvin 127
Torrey, Lorraine K 129
Torrey, Marjorie 129
Torrey, Pearl Evangeline 129
Torrey, Ralph Renville 128
Torrey, Robert 130
Torrey, Roy Leslie 128
Turner, Benjamin Rutherford 62
Turner, Mary Agnes 62
Tyler, Anderson 143

V
Vatnor, Anna 137
Vator, Anna 133
Veloske, Catherine 129

W
Wagner, Cecilia Elizabeth 156
Wagner, Dorothy M 159
Wagner, George Joseph 156
Wagner, Johann 156
Wagner, John 38
Wagner, Martha Frances 38
Wagner, Martin 39
Wagner, Mary Elizabeth 156
Wagner, Veronica 156
Wagner, William Kimball 159
Wagner, William Valentine 156
Waller, Catherine 86
Weber, Anna Maria 110
Weber, Anton 154
Weber, Mary 67
Weingart, Alfred 103
Weingart, Nicholas Simon 110
Wencel, Cleova Carlita 138
Wencel, Daryl Eugene 144
Wencel, Frank John 144
Wencel, Frederick Edward 144
Wencel, Glory Helen 144
Wencel, Joy Yvonne 144
Wencel, Lamoyne Edward 144
Wetor, Anna 133
Wicke, Alice Louellen 82
Wicke, Betty Ann 82
Wicke, Catherine Gladys 82
Wicke, Ernst 82
Wicke, Frederick John 82
Wicke, Joan Marie 82
Wicke, Joyce M. 82
Wicke, Leo 82
Wielowski, Catherine 129
Wienke, Henry Raymond 96
Wienke, Mary Elizabeth 96
Wienke, Raymond 96
Wienke, William Joseph 96
Wild, John Louis 157
Winkels, Theodore 87
Wormley, Dorothy 88
Wormley, Jesse 87
Wormley, Mary 87

Y-Z
Yonker, Elizabeth 157
Zarnstorff, Jack 50
Zimmerman, Herman 58
Zimmerman, Lois 58

Blue=Grandchildren; Red=Great-grandchildren; Green=2x Great-grandchildren

Reader's Notes

www.ingramcontent.com/pod-product-compliance
Lightning Source LLC
LaVergne TN
LVHW061634070526
838199LV00071B/6668